rüffer & rub visionaries

Johannes Dieterich, Ed.

TONY RINAUDO
– THE –
FOREST-
MAKER

Translations from German (texts by Johannes Dieterich
and Günter Nooke, and appendix) and proofreading
by Suzanne Kirkbright.

The author and publisher wish to thank the
Elisabeth Jenny Foundation for its generous support,
and special thanks go to **World Vision Germany**
for making it possible for Tony Rinaudo and Johannes
Dieterich to travel to Niger.

rüffer&rub Sachbuchverlag is supported by the
Federal Office of Culture, Switzerland, from 2016 to 2020.

Originally published as *Tony Rinaudo – Der Waldmacher*
Copyright © 2018 by rüffer & rub Sachbuchverlag GmbH, Zurich

All rights of the English edition:

First edition June 2018
All rights reserved
Copyright © 2018 by rüffer & rub Sachbuchverlag GmbH, Zurich
info@ruefferundrub.ch | www.ruefferundrub.ch

Typeface: Filo Pro
Printing and binding: Books on Demand GmbH, Norderstedt
Paper: Cream white, 90 g/m²

ISBN 978-3-906304-36-6

Preface | *Anne Rüffer* 6

Prologue | *Johannes Dieterich* 9
Tony's Travails | *Johannes Dieterich* 16
Discovering the Underground Forest | *Tony Rinaudo* 50
FMNR Is Now a Widely Scaled-Up Agricultural Practice
    in the Drylands: A Robust Legacy of Tony Rinaudo's
    Career | *Dennis Garrity* 92
"Trust Would Be a Good Starting Point" | *Interview with*
    Günter Nooke 126
Postscript | *Tony Rinaudo* 139

Appendix 144
Bibliography 145
List of Photos and Diagrams 148
About the Authors 149

Preface

Anne Rüffer, publisher

December 2, 2015, Geneva. SRO (standing room only) in the city's Auditorium Ivan Pictet. Thronging it is a group of distinguished persons. They have come to honor the four winners of this year's Alternative Nobel Prizes. The auditorium's building bears the name "Maison de la Paix"—"home of peace". Rarely has the name of the venue for an event so closely accorded with its thrust. The event is kicked off by two speakers: Barbara Hendricks, who is Germany's minister of the environment, and Michael Møller, who is Director-General at the UN in Geneva. The event's title is "On the front lines and in the courtrooms: forging human security".

The discussion following the two speeches is conducted by the four winners. Suddenly, one of them, Dr. Gino Strada, makes a statement of electrifying import. He states: "The UN was founded in the aftermath of the Second World War. Its purpose was and is to liberate following generations from being hostages of unceasing warfare. Since that day, the world has experienced more than 170 armed conflicts. And you have never broached the subject of how to abolish warfare? Come on guys, this is incredible!" The audience responds with embarrassed laughter and incredulous amazement.

Gino Strada knows all too well what he is talking about. In 1994, he founded "Emergency". This NGO provides medical treatment—often supplied at clinics built by Emergency itself—in regions roiled by conflict, and, as well, development assistance to victims of warfare. Of them, 10% are soldiers themselves—with the remaining 90% being civilians. Strada ends his statement with "You can call me a Utopian if you like. But remember, everything appears to be a Utopia until someone realizes it."

"I have a dream." Made by Dr. Martin Luther King, this statement is probably the one the most often quoted over the last few decades. That's because Dr. King's dream of a world in which justice prevails is shared by so many people. Some of them—more than we are probably aware of and yet not enough by far—have devoted themselves to employing their guts, their hearts and their minds to making this dream come true. Along with Dr. King and Gino Strada, other well-known "dreamers" include Mother Teresa and Jody Williams. Calling them "Utopians" is actually anything but an insult. Each great advance recorded by humanity started out as a Utopian idea, a hope, a vision.

This book is the second in our new series of "rüffer&rub visionaries". We have a very clear objective in launching it. These books are going to fan the sparks emanating from the ideas and hopes propagated by these visionaries into bonfires of dedication and endeavor. The heart of each book is the author's very personal look at her or his—highly-important—scientific, cultural or societal topic.

Each author will tell—in simple, inspiring words—how she or he got involved with this topic, and how she or he started looking for answers to its questions that made sense, for solutions dealing with its problems. These books will tell you what it means to commit yourself to a cause, to live your commitment every day, to develop and implement a vision for its realization. These visions are highly variegated—political, scientific or spiritual—in nature. All of them share their visionaries' yearning for a better world—and their willingness to put their hearts and souls into realizing them.

All of these visions and all of the activities undertaken to make them come true share something else in common: the deep-rooted conviction that we can positively shape our future, that we can restore the health of the planet on which we all live. Another strong conviction adhered to by all of us: we are convinced that each and every one of us is capable of undertaking the steps required to make each of us part of the solution, and not of the problem.

Prologue

Johannes Dieterich

Up to 700 million people could be obliged to leave their homelands during the next three decades because of the rapid pace of desertification in the landscapes where they live. This is no prophecy of doom made by an attention-seeking apocalyptic luminary, but rather the forecast from over a hundred scientists who convened in March 2018 in the Columbian capital Bogotá. In their joint report, experts of the Bonn-based Intergovernmental Science-Policy Platform on Biodiversity and Ecosystem Services (IPBES) state that by 2050 climate change and land destruction threatens to halve agricultural yields across vast swathes of the world. As a result, we must expect social destabilization and violent conflicts for the growing shortage of natural resources.

Admittedly, the shocking scenario also caught me off guard—even after more than 20 years living in Africa, I was unaware of the scale of the desertification of arable and pasture lands on the continent. When I met Tony Rinaudo for the first time in March 2016 it was not because I was chasing apocalyptic scenarios but part of my search for a 'positive story' from Africa which my editors in Germany are requesting with growing frequency. In view of the misery in other parts of the world, there is now a greater appetite for encouraging news from the continent once afflicted by diseases, wars and disasters. Rinaudo admirably fulfilled the expectations of him: the forest-maker made his mark as a champion of hope.

One could easily write a heroic tale based on his story: the selfless missionary turned successful campaigner against the desertification of entire landscape. But this would not do him any favours. Instead of being glorified Tony Rinaudo prefers to make himself dispensable. The agronomist believes that his mission will only be fulfilled when his idea has turned into a 'movement'. And when millions of people are self-motivated to stop cutting down trees on their fields and to get back to an integrated method of farming. That this paradigm change is feasible without massive efforts is the most intriguing aspect of Rinaudo's discovery. To make the degraded landscapes flourish again requires neither vast sums of money nor undue exertion.

Being on the road with Tony Rinaudo was one of the most impressive experiences of my travels on the continent. I have rarely encountered a pale-faced human being who is so 'in tune' with the African population. Arrogance is as alien to him as cynicism—or the patronizing attitude, which is the cardinal sin of so many white expat helpers. Tony suffers just the same as a smallholder farmer whose goat died; and he shares in his joy when his 'Apple of the Sahel' tree bears its first fruits. And all this is in 'Hausa', the colloquial dialect of West Africa that the Australian speaks like 'a donkey from Kano', as his conversational partners complement.

Rinaudo and his method of Farmer Managed Natural Regeneration (FMNR) are the central theme of this book. In the opening report, I describe my journeys with the 'forest-maker' to Ethiopia, Somaliland and Niger, where Rinaudo discovered the 'underground forest' almost 35 years ago. Rinaudo then gives a personal account of how he developed the FMNR method and demonstrated its benefits to the local farmers. In his contribution, the agronomist Dennis Garrity discusses the scientific facts about FMNR. And finally, Günter Nooke, German Chancellor Angela Merkel's Personal Representative for Africa, talks in an interview about the political ramifications of the forest-maker's discovery.

According to the scientists gathered in Bogotá, there is only one hope in the light of the rapidly advancing land destruction: namely, that local farmers can be convinced of 'sustainable land management'. Tony Rinaudo reckons that he has found the appropriate method for this kind of ecological management with FMNR—and just in time to stop the destruction of our livelihood or even being able to reverse it. While the former missionary personally experienced his discovery as a religious revelation, an agnostic is reminded of the saying by the German romantic poet Friedrich Hölderlin: 'But where danger threatens / That which saves from it also grows.' (*'Wo aber Gefahr ist, wächst das Rettende auch.'*)

For updated information about the FMNR method, training and educational films as well as success stories, please visit http://fmnrhub.com.au

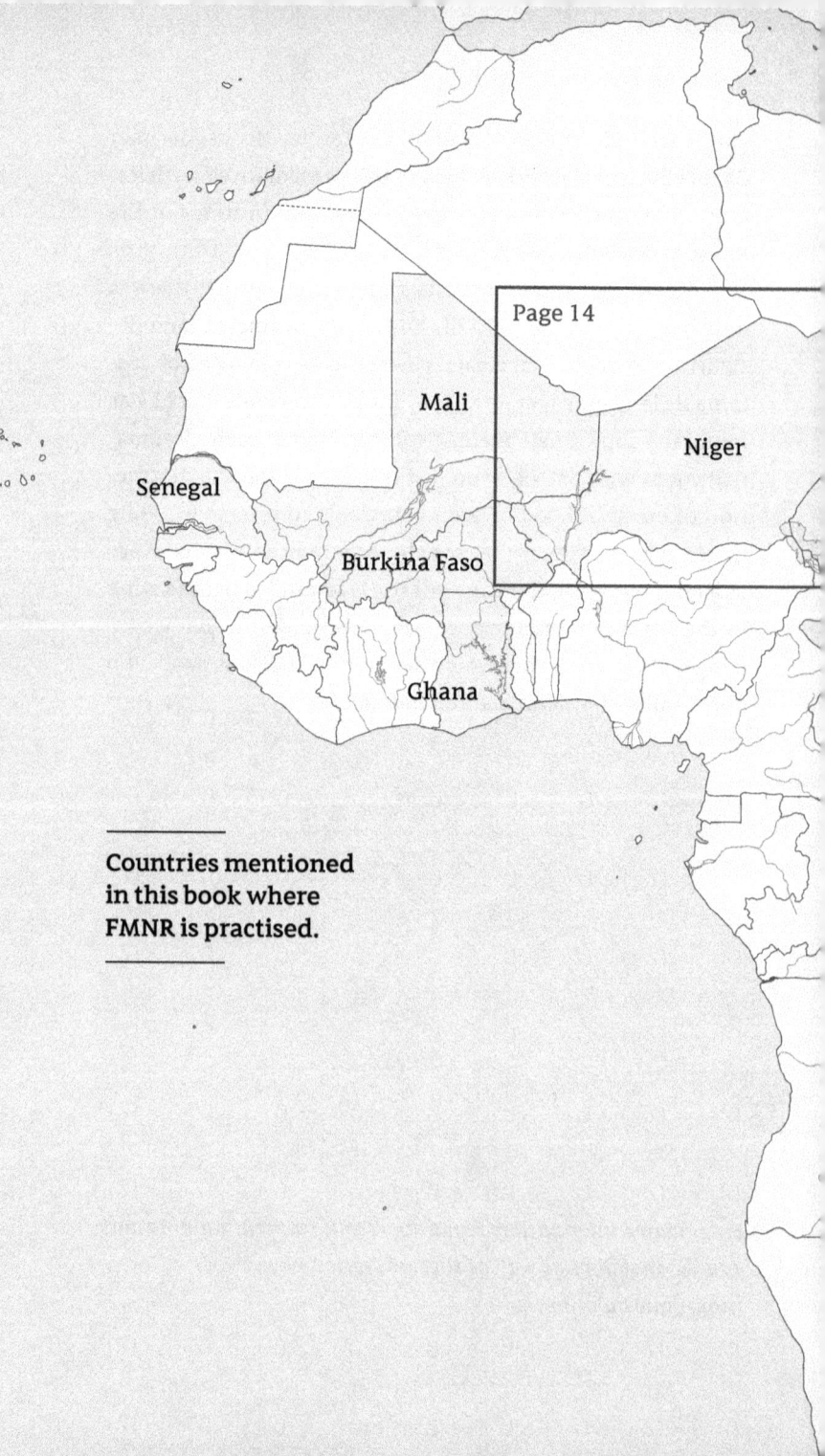

Countries mentioned in this book where FMNR is practised.

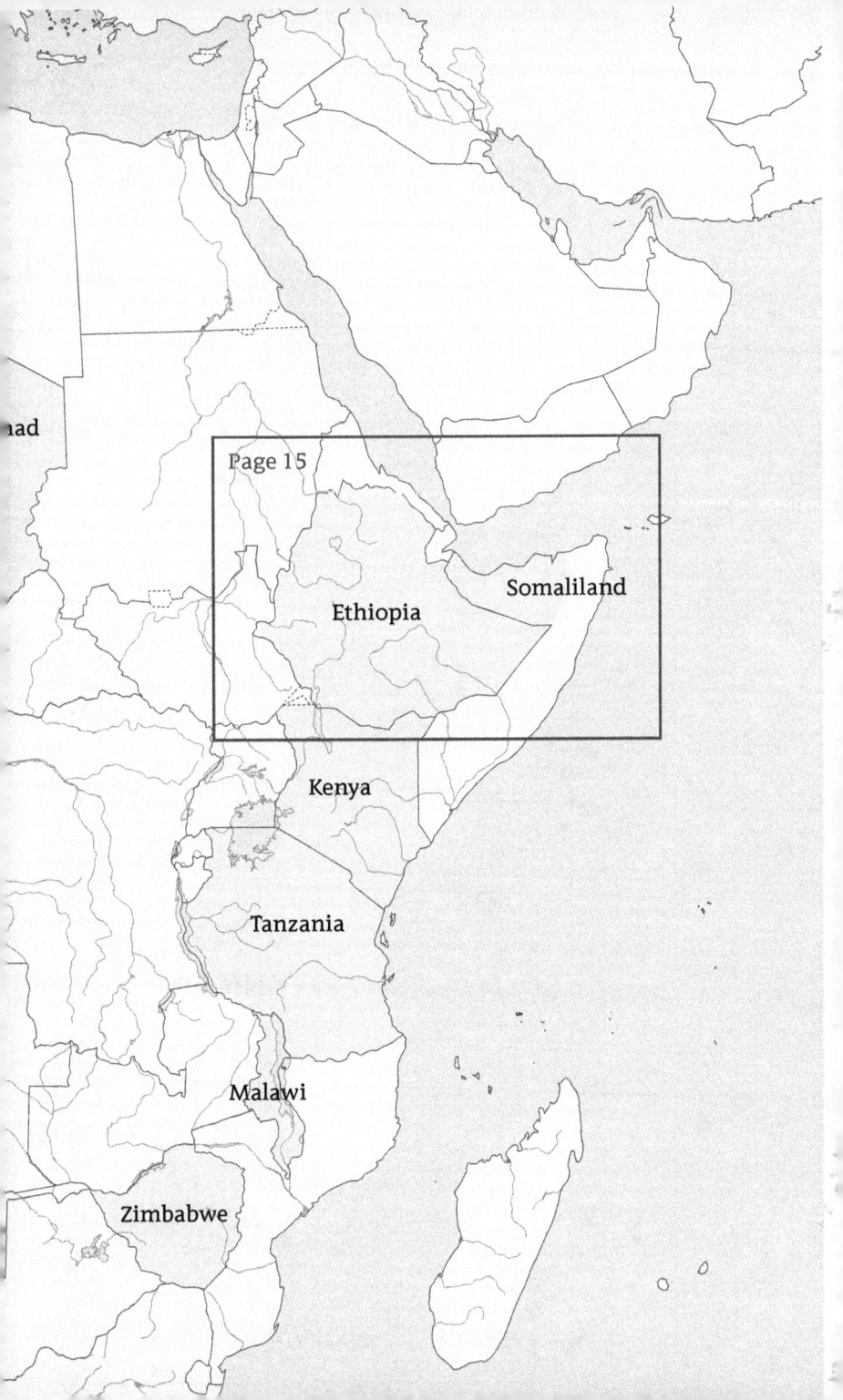

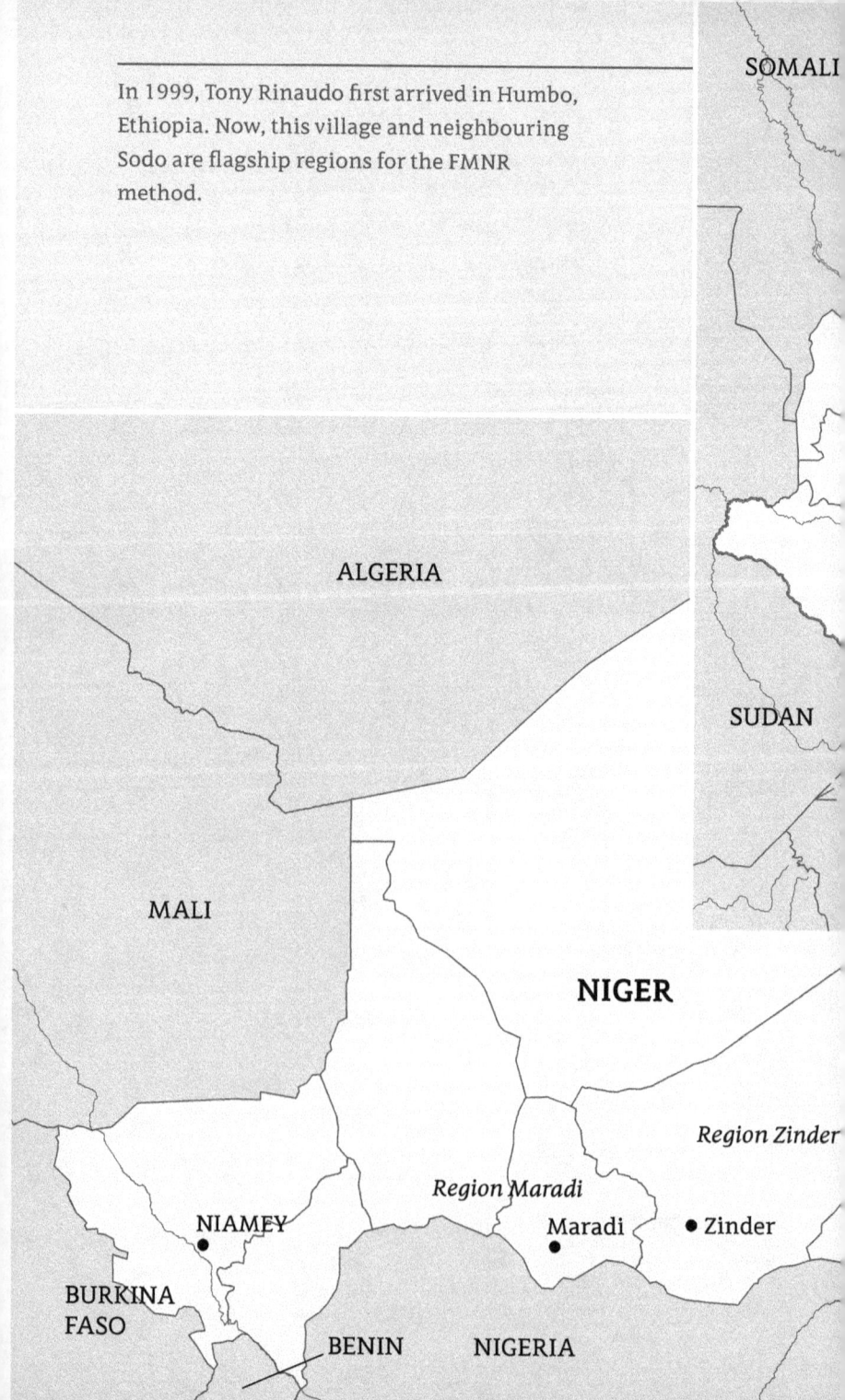

In 1999, Tony Rinaudo first arrived in Humbo, Ethiopia. Now, this village and neighbouring Sodo are flagship regions for the FMNR method.

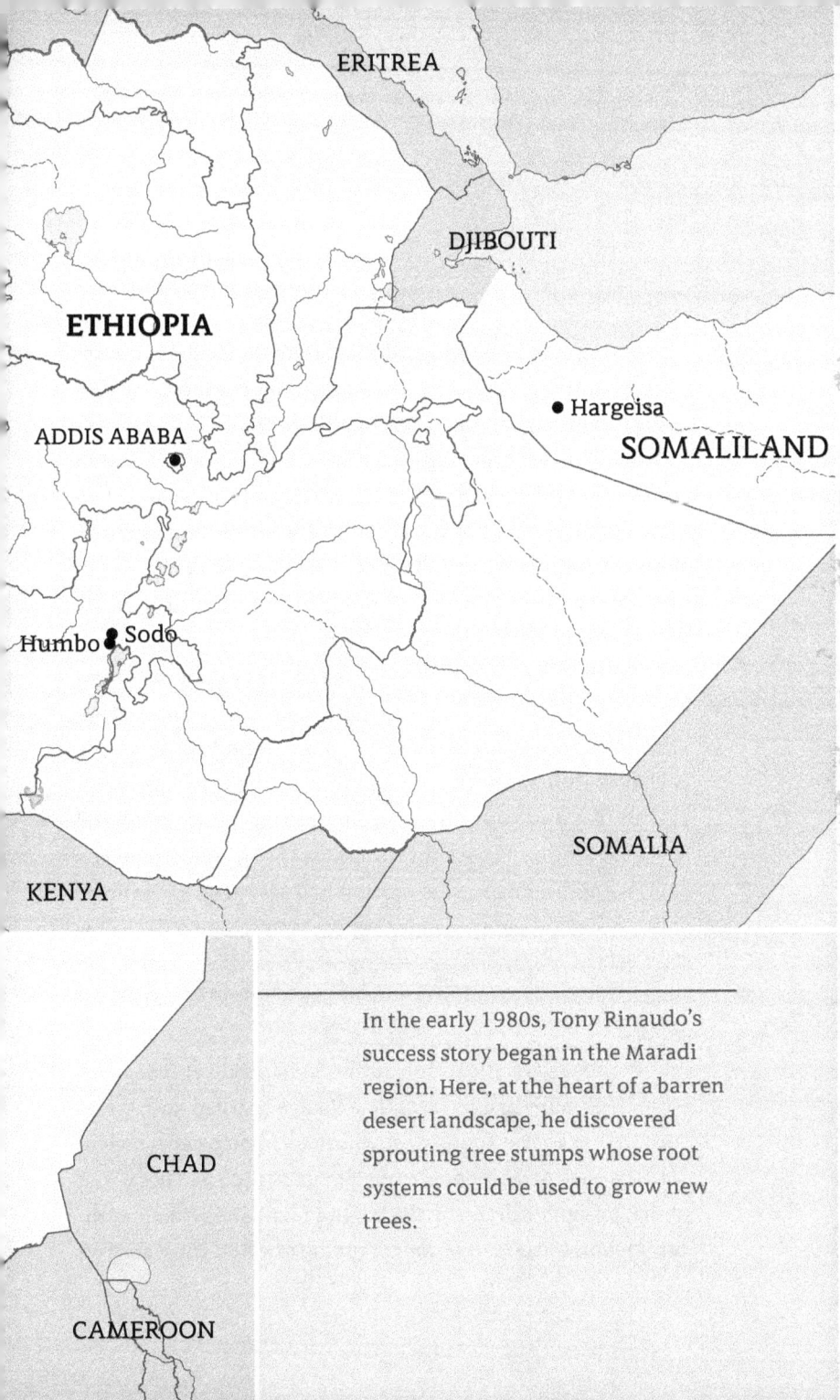

In the early 1980s, Tony Rinaudo's success story began in the Maradi region. Here, at the heart of a barren desert landscape, he discovered sprouting tree stumps whose root systems could be used to grow new trees.

Tony's Travails

Johannes Dieterich

The setting could easily be a film location for "Heidi". A mountain stream burbles along cheerfully. The cows contentedly munch on the lush grass. Resting his chin on his shepherd's crook, a boy gazes dreamily into the valley. Only his dark skin reveals that this is in fact not Heidi's homeland. Nearby, two grass-covered huts are the final giveaway that this picture-postcard scene is on a different continent, far away from Switzerland. We are in Africa, or more precisely: we are in the mountains near the southern Ethiopian city of Sodo.

"If you had been here ten years ago, you would have been even more astonished," says Tony Rinaudo. The Australian agriculture specialist seems ready to burst with joy. When the Melburnian first arrived in Sodo in 2006 the mountains still looked like a natural disaster zone. Instead of the trees and grass the landscape back then was mostly covered with thorny bushes and trailing plants. Erosion had carved deep channels into the slopes. The mudslides regularly raced down the valley during heavy rainfall, even tearing away several African round huts. On one occasion, a family of five was buried under the mud.

In those days, the people in the Sodo region still depended on food aid—like in Humbo, a village situated 50 kilometres further to the south-west whose local mountain resembled the back of a hippopotamus. Tony Rinaudo had been sent at that point to Humbo by the development and relief organization World Vision to support capping one of the last springs that was still flowing. Yet, the expert quickly realized that the local population here had a much more severe problem than the non-enclosed spring: they had destroyed their livelihood by constantly cutting down trees and overgrazing the pastureland.

"We often talked about whether we should move away," recalls Anato Katmar, whose three hectares of farmland lies at the foot of what was once the hippo's humpback mountain. "But where to?" Then, he was still living with his wife and their five children in a cramped, small hut. The corn and sorghum harvest yields deteriorated every year and sometimes massive boulders rolled down the bare mountainsides into his fields, burying and crushing the crops. From higher up, the only sound echoing down the mountain slope was that of the surviving animals—the mocking cries of the baboons. The monkeys devoured every piece of vegetation that was still sprouting on the barren slope. On many evenings in the year, the Katmars went to bed hungry.

Ethiopia is considered as the continent's prime land of famine. At one time, this state on the Horn of Africa—now with a population of over 100 million—recorded the worst drought disasters on the planet.

Until 1984, when Bob Geldof's "Band Aid" shook the world's conscience out of its lethargy, half a million Ethiopians had to perish. Even today, like most of the continent's 55 countries, Ethiopia has difficulty feeding its population. And while the number of those starving has fallen worldwide over the past 25 years, in Africa it has continued to rise: from 181.7 million in 1990 to 232.5 million in 2017.

Besides the political and climatic causes of the chronic crisis, there are also ecological factors contributing—primarily, the soil deterioration and the disappearance of trees. Ethiopia, which was once covered with vast areas of woodland, has lost almost 90% of its woody plants over the past 50 years. Yet, if the experts agree on one thing then it is the importance of trees for the soil quality: they keep the soil fertile and moist, their shade considerably reduces soil temperatures and, as windbreaks, they prevent the desiccated, dust-like earth in the dry season from scattering far and wide.

Ecological devastation has plagued the Sahel region the worst. Until twenty years ago, the desert here was expanding further and further southwards and the trees had vanished. Nearly all attempts to control the growing effects of erosion in the arid zones, by planting new trees, ended in failure: most of the costly seedlings didn't even survive their first birthday. "Millions of US-dollars were wasted," says Tony Rinaudo, who previously managed a small reforestation programme in the Sahel region. "The extremely low survival rates of planted trees was a bitter pill to swallow."

However, now this is history, observes the otherwise remarkably modest Australian. The agronomist from Melbourne believes that he has discovered a substantially more successful method of reforestation and soil revitalization—and one that involves zero costs. Rinaudo has undertaken nothing less than to put a stop to hunger in Africa. His discovery could be more significant for the continent than billions of US-dollars of development aid.

"Get me out of here!"

When the Australian first arrived in Humbo in 1999, he was not greeted like the Messiah. The village residents were not exactly hostile to the overseas agriculturalist, but they were certainly sceptical. They suspected that the pale-faced guest was on a mission to sell their land to investors. Besides, his suggestions sounded ridiculous or even suspicious when he talked about letting trees grow on their valuable fields, keeping starving cattle from the bare slopes for a time, or preventing the charcoal burners from cutting down every last tree. The people preferred to have nothing to do with the curious tree-hugger. Anato Katmar was among the few who were prepared to give the foreigner a chance—possibly because he no longer had anything to lose anyway. "Tony", says Katmar, "was my last hope." For his first cooperative, Rinaudo had to make do with a handful of farmers, and besides that they were also exposed to the ridicule and mistrust of their neighbours.

Today, there are seven cooperatives in Humbo with over five thousand members. None of them seems to doubt Tony Rinaudo's method any more. While in the El Niño year of 2016 the region's other villages were dependent again on food aid, the cooperatives at the foot of the hippo's humpback mountain produced food surpluses that are at times sold to the UN's World Food Programme (WFP) to distribute to those parts of the country in need. The mountain is now covered again with woodland trees that grow above a height of two metres; and the thriving fruit trees on the farms not only give shade and fruit, but occasionally, pruned branches for firewood. Meanwhile, instead of his round hut Anato has managed to afford a real house constructed from bricks and a corrugated iron roof. Apart from the standard corn and sorghum (millet), he also cultivates coffee and bananas, which he sells with the mangos from the garden at the local market. The farmer invested his revenue in his children's education: his two oldest children have already finished their studies, while the three youngest still attend grammar school. The Katmar family currently enjoys three meals a day. "Hunger," says Papa Anato, "is now consigned to our memories."

Tony Rinaudo follows the account of his model farmer with a beaming expression—in Humbo, a dream is being fulfilled for the agronomist. In the early 1980s, Rinaudo was sent to Niger by his organization "Serving in Mission" (SIM). His job there was to stop the advance of the desert by planting new trees. For several years, the Australian behaved like a Don Quixote of the seedlings in his fight against the mills of the sandstorms that were devastating the land. Scarcely 10 % of little trees had survived the heat and dust storms after planting, he recalls. If one of the seedlings did survive, it was later eaten by the goats or finally cut down by people for firewood. Finally, Rinaudo might have lost his faith as well as his patience: "Get me out of here!", he quarrelled like Job with his god.

In the eyes of the former missionary, his story in Maradi continued in a biblical connotation. One day, as Rinaudo stopped to let the air pressure out of the tyres of his off-road vehicle to travel more easily through the loose sand, it was as if the scales fell from his eyes. The green shoots, which were sprouting all around him in the sand, were by no means useless weeds—as he had always assumed beforehand. Rather, on closer inspection he saw that they were trees sprouting from their stumps. However, if these sprouts could grow so vigorously in the sand, an intact root system must be supporting them, concluded Rinaudo. As the same phenomenon could be observed across the region, he could assume that there was a vast network of roots spreading beneath the sand of the Sahel zone: an underground forest with roots resembling the branches of trees stuck into the earth upside down. The significance of this observation was not lost on him. He immediately realized that this vast root system made the need for ineffectual tree planting redundant. The underground forest was the key to success.

His Damascus road experience turned Rinaudo's world upside down as well—from its head to its feet, as Karl Marx would have said. If the little green shoots in the sand were given a chance, they would grow into trees of their own accord, he speculated: all that was needed for the regeneration of the devastated landscape was a penknife, which Rinaudo always carries with him and uses to trim back the shoots of the young trees that grow more like bushes. As the sprouting trees can draw on the nutrients that are still stored in the root system, particularly sugar, they usually grow into mature trees at a breathtaking pace. He has often seen how in three years a weak, sprouting stump becomes a five-metre tall tree, explains the Australian.

City of disused petrol stations

Maradi must be the city with the world's highest number of petrol stations per resident. The filling stations on the arterial routes of the Nigerien provincial city are lined up like telegraph posts. However, most of them are not in use. They exist thanks to a Nigerien governmental ruling which states that only the owners of a petrol station are granted a fuel export licence for the neighbouring country of Nigeria. Obviously, the local border traffic facilitates such high earnings that the costs of building a useless station are very quickly paid off. This is one example of the bizarre bureaucracy which the almost 17 million residents of the West African state must negotiate in their daily life.

Otherwise, Maradi is like any other provincial city in these latitudes: too hot, too dusty and yet full of activity around the clock. The drivers of the ubiquitous motorcycle taxis only spend the fiercest midday heat sprawled across the tank of their Chinese machines, while vintage Peugeot 404s still clatter along the mostly unpaved streets and old men seated on large stones pass the time playing board games. The only lush green in the otherwise sand-coated city is in the stadium with its artificial grass funded by FIFA. Now and then, cattle herders from the surrounding area move in to the seemingly lush pasture with their livestock, city dwellers scornfully report: only to find out that the fresh grass in the football arena is in fact plastic. Otherwise, there is not much for the city residents to laugh about. In Maradi, not even half of those looking for paid work have a job. Most of the almost one million residents must make do with the equivalent of one euro per day. Their corrugated iron huts usually have neither running water nor electricity.

The Sahel zone is the stepchild of the continent whose basic conditions are dysfunctional: in the strip of land measuring only a few hundred kilometres wide, and stretching from Senegal in the west of the territory to East African Sudan, poverty seems to be deeper rooted than the wild fig tree with its 120-metres deep shoots. The Sahel zone is the source of a high number of migrants who seek their fortune on the neighbouring European continent, despite the perilous journey. Here, enraged Islamists find it easy to recruit new fighters—they regard the influence of the Christian world rulers as at least one cause of their misery. Not far from Maradi, the Nigerian sect Boko Haram spreads its terror—the name 'boko' meaning 'Western education' and 'haram' meaning 'sin'. In northern Niger, members of the "al-Qaeda in the Islamic Maghreb" terrorist group are active. Western armed forces regard the Sahel region as such dangerous territory that they have stationed thousands of their soldiers here. However, the French, American and German army commanders also know that the true causes of the danger cannot be dealt with by armed force. It is the poverty, which must be conquered, and this is Tony Rinaudo's vocation.

Speaking 'Hausa' like a donkey from Kano

"Tony, Tony!", calls an older man, as he recognizes the pale-faced passenger in the vehicle on the outskirts of Dan Indo village. The vehicle is soon surrounded by a swarm of young people and about a dozen laughing men. Despite his now grey-tinged hair, everyone instantly recognizes the former missionary—they clap their hands, embrace and shake their heads in disbelief. An imposing man introduces himself as Tony too: his parents named him after the Australian over thirty years ago. This is not the only dark-skinned Tony in Maradi district, as it emerges during our visit. Judging by the popularity of his name alone, Rinaudo must have achieved outstanding work here.

Sule Lebo, the village elder in Dan Indo, has no intention of letting go of his visitor's hand again. The two are deep in conversation in Lebo's native language, Hausa, which repeatedly makes him burst into loud peals of laughter. "He can still speak it!", the mayor slaps his knees. Tony speaks Hausa "like a donkey from Kano", we often hear during the next few days. Apparently, this is meant as a compliment.

After the overjoyed greeting, however, Sule Lebo quickly gets to the point. Things have been tough in recent years, explains the village chief. The rains failed abysmally, the harvests were miserable and finally the 63-year-old also had to have an operation on his prostate which cost an equivalent EUR 400. To pay the school money for his children, Lebo was forced to sell three of his eight oxen—and still the farmer and his two wives and 17 children are doing much better today than in the early 1980s, when he got to know Rinaudo. While Lebo only farmed three hectares of land back then, today he farms 22 hectares. He used to harvest only 150 kilograms of millet per hectare, while now it is 500 kilograms. And his wife's 20 goats and sheep didn't exist in those days. When the Australian agronomist started work here, Lebo goes on to say, there was scarcely a tree to be seen between the village and the paved road almost two kilometres away. Today, there are hundreds of trees scattered across the fields.

The village chief was one of the few who gave Rinaudo a chance at that time. Dan Indo was one of the first villages included in the projects managed by the foreign expert. The field trial could hardly have gone any better. Within just a few short years, plenty of trees had sprouted on the fields belonging to the village residents—they gave shade, reduced the soil temperature, acted as windbreaks and as a by-product even produced timber for building huts or for firewood. The proceeds from Lebo's harvest tripled and meanwhile his annual earnings, from the sale of timber alone, are about EUR 130—that's a considerable sum by Nigerien standards. Thanks to his many fields, the oxen, goats and chickens the subsistence farmer has fulfilled his ambition to become a diversified farmer. Lebo laughs that next to the Almighty he only has to thank Tony for this.

There are many nuances to the situation that emerges while touring the villages in a 30-kilometre radius north of Maradi. In Waye Kai, by his own admission the village chief Dan Lamso manages "so many trees", that he could "not even count them any longer". As a mark of his gratitude, he hands Rinaudo two cockerels that land with loud protests on the loading platform of our hired vehicle. Scarcely 20 kilometres further on and the mood is already slightly more depressed: here, in the past two years the number of trees in the villagers' fields has been drastically reduced. To compensate for the lost harvests because of the drought, the smallholder farmers sold large quantities of wood. At least, this is how they managed to make ends meet without too much hardship, Rinaudo consoles himself. "Trees can be like a savings account that you can live on when times are hard."

Rinaudo seems irritated by the conditions in Sarkin Hatsi where right at the beginning of the visit a woman comes up to him begging. "Go back to your field and look after the plants and trees, then you don't need to beg," the petitioner is told. The former missionary has no intention of distributing charity handouts, instead he wants to change the conditions. "Isn't that Tony?", a man with his arm in a sling calls from the neighbouring house. Damani Idi injured his shoulder in a fall from the roof. The 58-year-old turns out to be one of Rinaudo's former star pupils. He cultivated hundreds of acacias on his fields and made coffee out of their seeds. However, Idi explains that he has now closed his roastery: his sieve broke down. "Oh, nonsense!", protests Rinaudo. A new sieve could cost a few euros at the most. Then he was simply too lazy, the farmer stalls any more questions—obviously, the father of 13 children (of whom six have already died) is trying to avoid a lengthy discussion. Rinaudo says that to find out what is actually happening in the village, he would need much more time than he has available. At least, one thing is to be documented: not all the problems of a community can be solved with trees.

Tambara-Sofoua makes the best impression of all the villages during the visit. Here, the locals have even set up a community watchdog to protect themselves against tree thieves. Besides, an expert funded by World Vision has the job of further refining the rather long-named "Farmer Managed Natural Regeneration" (FMNR), the method made famous by Rinaudo. Currently, he is showing the smallholder farmers how grafting improved cultivars of *Ziziphus* onto regenerated wild *Ziziphus mauritania* trees. The fruit of this tree, known as the "Apple of the Sahel", can be sold for a good price at the market. In addition, WV is introducing modern beehives, now that there are enough regenerated trees to support the industry.

During his time in Maradi, Rinaudo also experimented with the introduction of non-domestic trees. Due to their rapid growth, their drought resistance and the nutrient-rich seeds, he especially liked the Australian *Acacia colei* which had already been brought into the country by the Niger Government. The smallholder farmers achieved great success with the seeds. Baro Yacouba from Kumbulla delighted his neighbours with acacia spaghetti and acacia pancakes. However, Rinaudo prefers not to discuss the subject, as some scientists heavily criticized his imports of trees. Hard-core invasive weed specialists argued that alien trees had no place in a non-native environment: This kind of "biological imperialism" would only spread disaster. Rinaudo finds the ideological debate appalling. In over 35 years there has been no 'alien acacia species' invasion as predicted, he counters. Rather, it has contributed to environmental restoration and brought great blessing to arguably the poorest people on earth.

Lakes in the desert

Dark clouds gather on the journey back to Maradi. Soon afterwards, it starts to rain torrentially—and this is still before the actual rainy season, which usually gets off to a quieter start. Rinaudo explains animatedly that he has never experienced such a cloudburst in Niger, while the semi-desert around us is transformed into a lakeland. In his time, rainfall happened mostly at night, the agriculturalist continues. During the daytime, there was probably "too much heat reflected" from the white sand which deflected the rain clouds. Rinaudo is convinced that the rising tree population has an effect on the climate: he had often seen how the clouds move across the heated open spaces, while they release their rain over the cooler woodland areas. Research in this context is still in its early stages. However, it now seems to be widely acknowledged that trees influence rainfall.

Tony Rinaudo is pleased that his visit coincides with the first rains of the season. This is how—jokingly, of course—he can boast about being the rain maker. Those who are familiar with the appearances in Africa of Western benefactors and self-professed experts, will appreciate Rinaudo's social grace among Africans: he is warm, yet funny, extremely polite and always modest. He has a special relationship with Joho, his former employee, whom he has engaged again as a driver for our tour. The two are doubled up with laughter, while they reminisce on the journey about old times—everything is discussed in Hausa, of course. Joho is proud of his white fellow passenger, the 'Nasarra'. He introduces him to strangers as a team member from the United Nations, or as an influential expert who has the ear of the president. Slightly uncomfortable, Rinaudo generously lets the stories pass.

Back in Maradi, a crowd of old friends is already waiting at the entrance to the mission headquarters. They want to shake Rinaudo's hand, introduce their son or ask for support with a grandchild's school education. Previously the compound was accessible to everybody, whereas now a two-metre high wall protects it. This is both due to the increasing crime as well as the deteriorating relations between radicalized Muslims and the small Christian minority. An angry crowd of people enraged by events elsewhere in the world had already wanted to set fire to the mission headquarters. Five missionaries from Australia and the US still live at the base. However, they are not involved in reforestation activities.

The next day, Rinaudo is due to attend the state radio station to participate in a live interview. The studio resembles a junk room that has not been tidied for years: roof trusses hang from the ceiling, hardly a single lamp functions properly, while a greasy layer of dust, like a brown sheet, has covered the furniture, equipment and floors. But the Australian guest is on top form. During the conversation, the studio team repeatedly erupts into resounding laughter. The exhilaration was largely because of his liberal use of Hausa proverbs, Rinaudo was later to explain. He had learned his Hausa with an old-fashioned textbook and through engaging with the older generation who had not lost the richness of their language.

Despite the studio's archaic electronics, the discussion seems to have filtered through somehow to the outside world. One farmer phones in after the next, and all of them offer praise for Rinaudo's FMNR method. According to surveys by World Vision, in Maradi district alone presently more than 1.2 million smallholder farmers practise the natural regeneration technique. Meanwhile, throughout the country 200 million trees now grow—instead of five million in the early 1980s. No wonder that Rinaudo is in an excellent mood after his studio interview: "I think that my dream has come true."

The Platinum Standard

In comparison to Maradi's sand-brown landscapes, the surrounding hills of the southern Ethiopian provincial city of Sodo are a green paradise. "It's the gold standard for our projects," says Tony Rinaudo. A few kilometres outside the small city, a cooperative set up with guidance from World Vision has planted some seedlings in a fenced-off area about the size of a football field. Beehives are situated alongside, where the buzzing noise is like the hum from beneath high-voltage power lines. Initially, they had only cultivated useful fuel-wood and timber trees here such as *Grevillea* and *Acacia*, explains the chairman of the cooperative, Berata Bassa. "Until we had the idea of the apple trees." Apple trees of all sizes are now dispersed across the area: some trees are scarcely a metre high, while others already have mature fruits. The fruit trees are an excellent product to sell, continues Bassa. Both the seedlings and their fruit are a good source of income by Ethiopian standards—one kilo of apples brings in the equivalent of almost one euro. The honey business is doing even better. You can receive almost EUR 2 per kilo for the bees' nectar. The head of the cooperative even tolerates the occasional bee sting—just now, one of the creatures sacrificed its life in revenge for the constant stealing of honey.

The screeching of baboons resonates from the other side of the valley—for the cooperative, the primates, along with leopards, eagles and warthogs, are the new problem children. Rinaudo remarks that the reforestation would also mean the return of the wild animals. They raid the crops of the smallholders, take a goat or calf and at times have harmed people. Some farmers suggested shooting the intruders. However, others have learned about the tourism value of wildlife. They now propose a small nature park. "It's a textbook case of development," says Rinaudo. "One achievement builds on the other."

The wild animals are only the most recent of a string of problems faced by communities working to restore the forest. Other problems were associated with people who made charcoal for a living. They had already cut down all the trees on Humbo's hippo humpback mountain. It goes without saying that they couldn't continue their destructive work under the auspices of "Farmer Managed Natural Regeneration". An alternative occupation had to be found for them. Working closely with community leaders, local government officials and forestry department personnel, World Vision identified the most vulnerable members of the community, including charcoal makers, then provided training and equipped them to run alternative enterprises. They could re-train as tailors or hairdressers and would also be provided with a small salon or sewing machine. Several years later, none of the former charcoal makers seems to regret the career change. Today, remarks 24-year-old Wadu Henok, he earns a great deal more with his tailor's shop than before: "And it's obviously much more fun."

Sodo and Humbo even surged from the gold to the platinum standard—by generating money through their reforestation successes. The Humbo project is registered with the Clean Development Mechanism (CDM), which is part of the Kyoto agreement, and the Sodo project sells its carbon credits on the voluntary market. Both schemes are international financial compensation mechanisms. Industrialized nations can team up with restoration initiatives in the developing world and can offset, or compensate for their greenhouse gas emissions by making payments to communities, which engage in reforestation activities. Payments are tied to the amount of carbon dioxide sequestered by the growing trees. The process is costly, bureaucratically complex and current carbon prices are low. These factors partially explain the low number of carbon trading reforestation projects around the world.

In the case of the Humbo CDM project, as of August 2017 the seven cooperatives managing the forest had received USD 554,681 since project inception—these are vast amounts by local standards. The money was invested in a grain store, a corn mill and irrigation systems. Cooperative members can also take out small loans. These investments provide sound building blocks for ongoing sustainable development which is already transforming the lives of the participants. "This is a wonderful outcome," comments Rinaudo. At the same time, he warns, though, against placing too much hope in carbon as a cash-generating machine: "That's only a distraction from the primary benefits of reforestation and can easily result in disappointment." Restored vegetation cover and ecosystems provide for free a platform for sustainable development into the future, irrespective of the whims of the carbon market.

In the meantime, Rinaudo's method is gradually spreading across the entire continent. Partnering with the World Agroforestry Centre, World Vision has co-hosted international FMNR conferences in Malawi and Kenya that were attended by interested participants from numerous African states. Hundreds of workshops have been conducted and information is freely available on the web. Awareness and knowledge of FMNR have now reached a point where it is the method of choice in discussions on large-scale reforestation across the continent. Today, FMNR is practised in more than 20 countries on the continent, including in arid Somaliland, which is an absolute hardship case. If the platinum standard is practised in Ethiopia, then we must talk about the sand standard in Somaliland. Here, one drought season rapidly follows the next, and with 200 millimetres of rainfall at the most, even in the normal years only half as much rain falls in the East African semi-desert region as in Niger. "If FMNR works here", remarks Rinaudo, "then it will work almost everywhere."

The sand standard

A small convoy of off-road vehicles races in the searing heat across terrain that resembles a moon landscape. During the eight-hour bumpy ride from Somaliland's capital city Hargeisa to the Red Sea there are as good as no trees and scarcely any green colouring to identify. Instead, more and more children stand begging by the side of the track for water, or there are goat and camel carcasses, for which any kind of help comes too late. Older residents of the former British colony remember that only a few decades ago trees grew and animals grazed on the hillsides of their internationally unrecognized land. However, long ago the charcoal makers cut down everything. With the exception of some insects, no wild animal can be seen here anymore. One of the few activities that Somalilanders could earn money from was by producing charcoal for the Saudi-Arabian market. Every year, the tree population dropped by 1% in the semi-desert state—almost twice as fast as the African average.

A fenced-off area emerges ahead of us; its man-high trees can already be identified from far off. The trial field doesn't exactly look like a blossoming landscape. Nevertheless, the carefully pruned tree shoots have continued to grow despite the drought years—grass grows between the bushes that the village residents need for fodder as well as for thatching their hut roofs. Beehives are also visible. Members of the cooperative earned around EUR 700 from the sale of honey in the previous year. However, now the swarms have dispersed far and wide because of the prolonged drought. "To our western eyes, this looks terrible", says Rinaudo. "But the trees are alive and will spring to life immediately with the onset of rains."

Just a few kilometres away, a lush green oasis suddenly emerges from the barren landscape. Here, Ibrahim Muse Elim is experimenting with the FMNR method. The 56-year-old farmer has groundwater which he pumps from a depth of ten metres. However, because of the drought every month he has to bore deeper. At the edge of his land, Ibrahim has set up a small greenhouse for seedlings. He keeps the goats away from the thorny branches with improvised fences and lets saplings grow in-between his vegetable beds. He used to believe that the trees would deprive his vegetables of nutrients, the farmer remarks. So, previously he didn't plant anything around them. This changed when Rinaudo showed him that at midday his unprotected soil reached temperatures exceeding 70 degrees, while the temperature is half that in the shade of a tree. Today, Ibrahim's harvest is almost twice as plentiful as it was before. His family eats three meals a day, all ten children go to school and recently he could even pay for his oldest child's wedding. Tony Rinaudo bends down to a bush and carefully cuts back the side shoots with his worn-down penknife. "When I hear stories like this," remarks the forest-maker, "then I feel happy."

Rinaudo Festival in the Nigerien Maradi region: Wherever the former missionary appears, he is met with rapturous calls "Tony, Tony!".

P. 34, bottom | In the Somali town of Hargeisa, he presents his re-greening plans in a workshop (below left).

P. 35, top | At the radio station in Maradi, he answers questions about his FMNR method—in fluent Hausa.

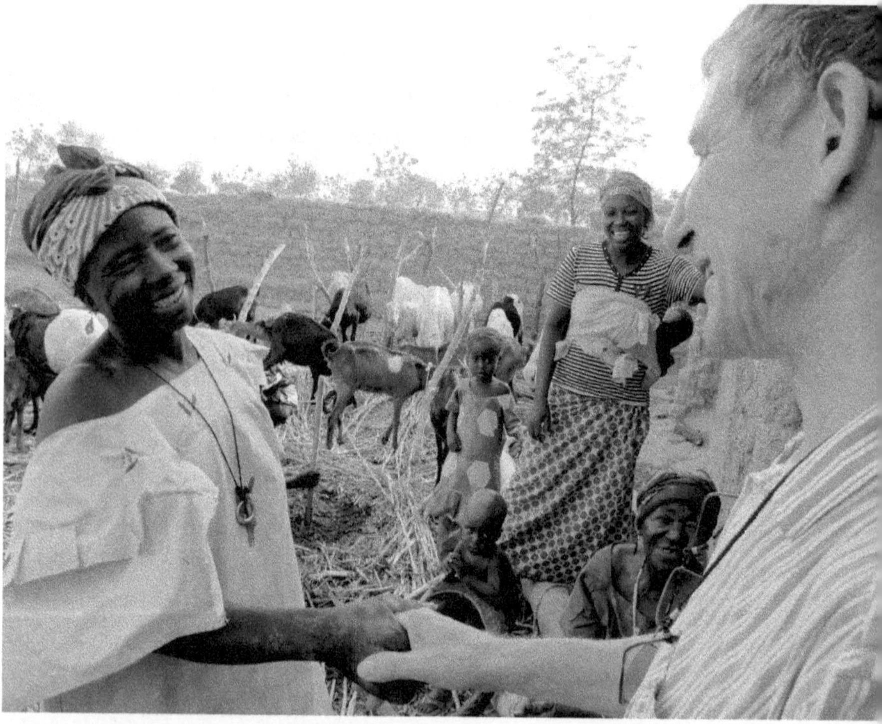

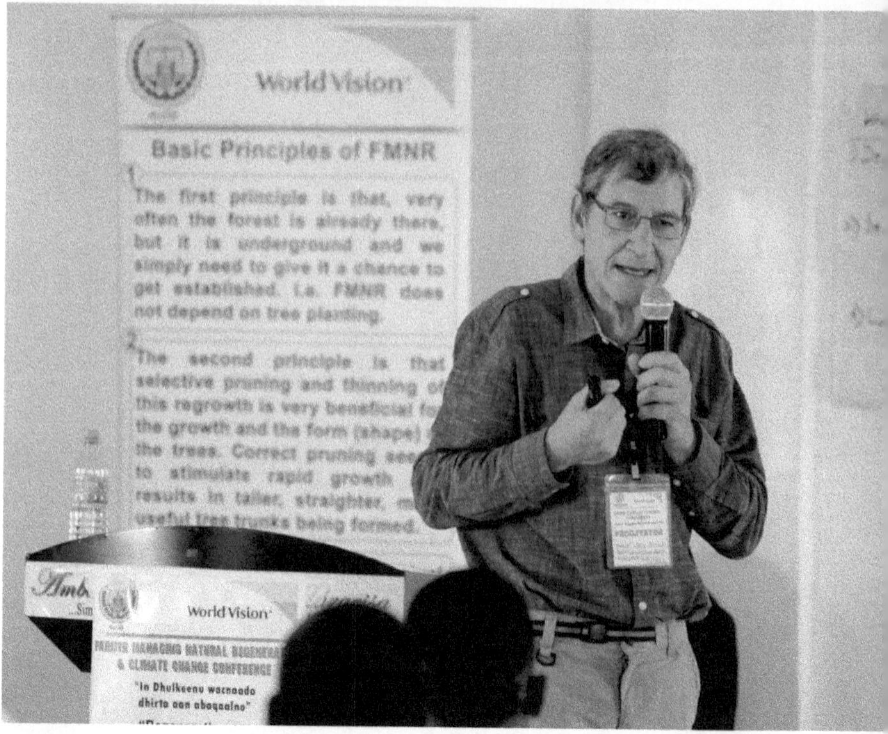
World Vision
Basic Principles of FMNR
1
The first principle is that, very often the forest is already there, but it is underground and we simply need to give it a chance to get established. i.e. FMNR does not depend on tree planting.
2
The second principle is that
selective pruning and thinning of
this regrowth is very beneficial fo
the growth and the form (shape)
the trees. Correct pruning see
to stimulate rapid growth
results in taller, straighter, m
useful tree trunks being formed.
World Vision
& CLIMATE CHANGE CONFERENCE
"In Dhulkeenu wacnaado dhirta oon aboqaalno"

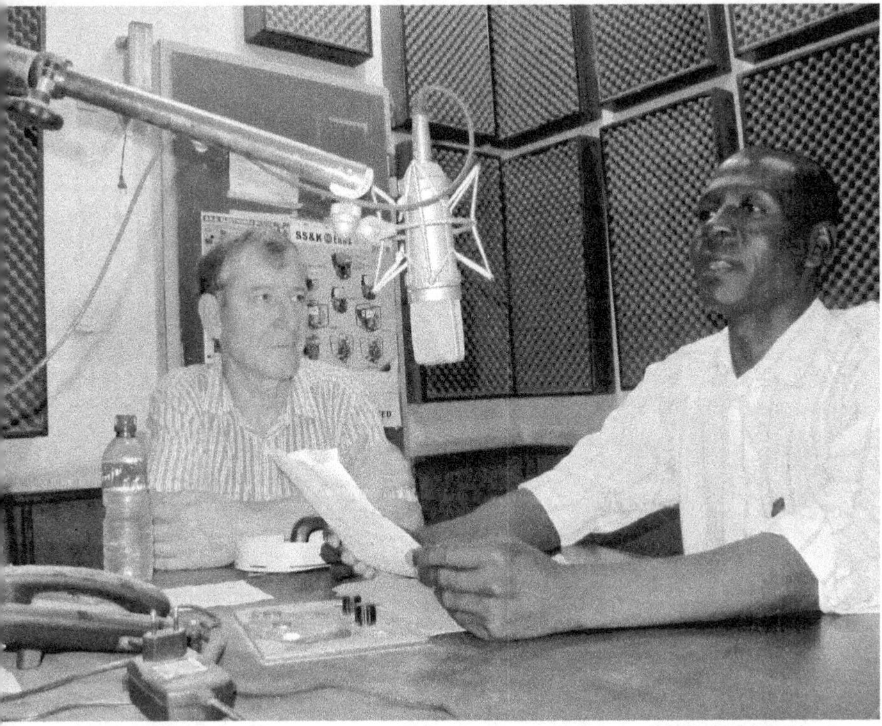

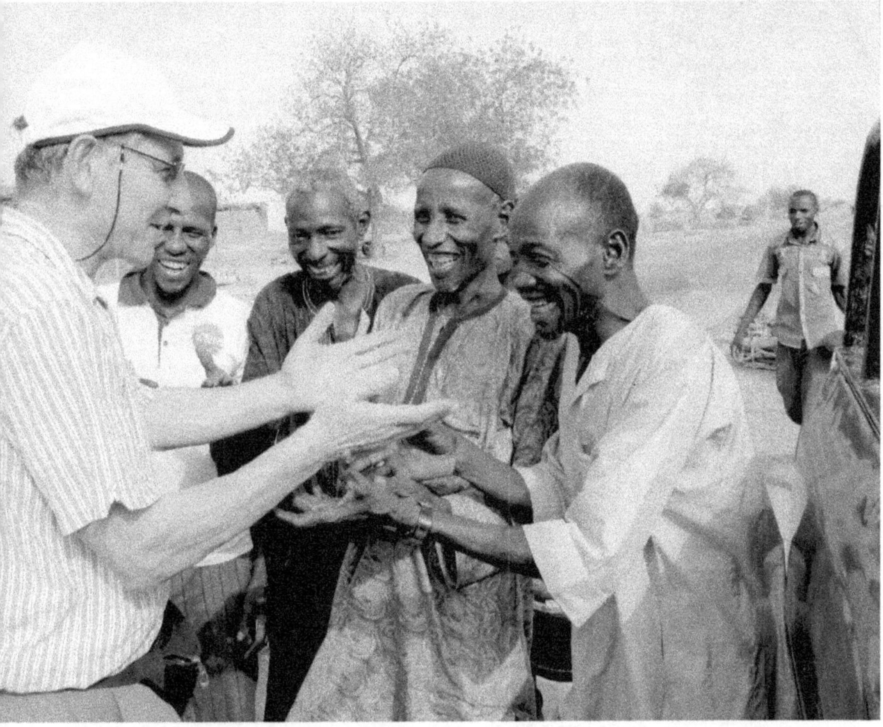

A pruning lesson: Tony Rinaudo explains to farmers from Tambara-Sofoua village in the Nigerien Maradi region how to handle tree shoots. For this purpose, he always carries his well-worn penknife in his trouser pocket.

Every tree was once a shrub: A farmer from the Nigerien village of Tambara-Sofoua grafts the shoot of an Apple of the Sahel tree onto a Jujube tree (top left), while the village chief, Sule Lebo, from Dan Indo shows his friend the latest successes with FMNR. Even in dust-dry north-eastern Somaliland, Tony Rinaudo doesn't give up hope (below left).

Humbo's hippo humpback mountain—
before the FMNR project start, 2006

Humbo's hippo humpback mountain—
six years after the project start, 2012

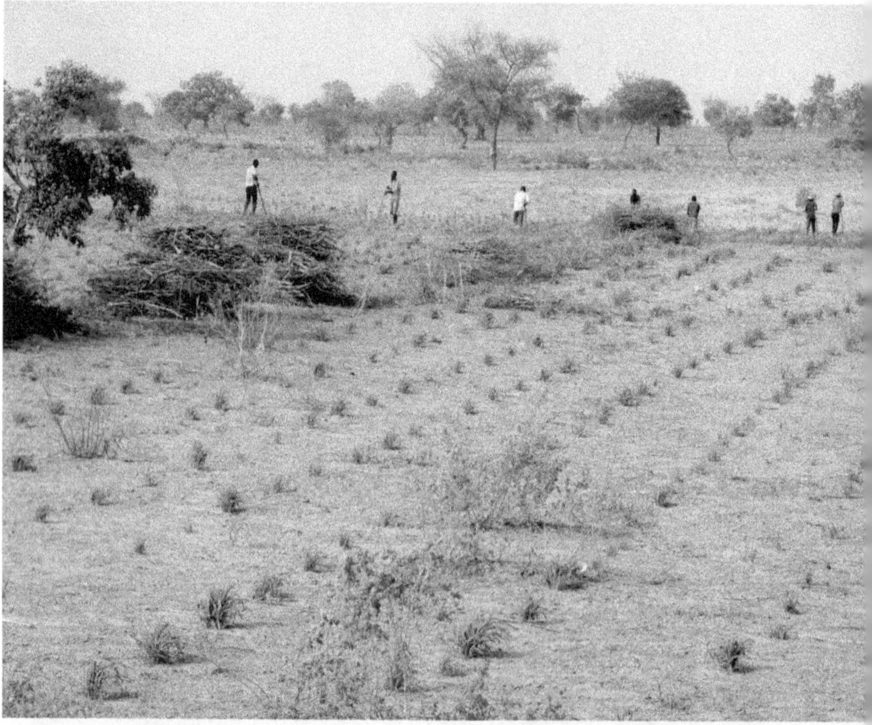

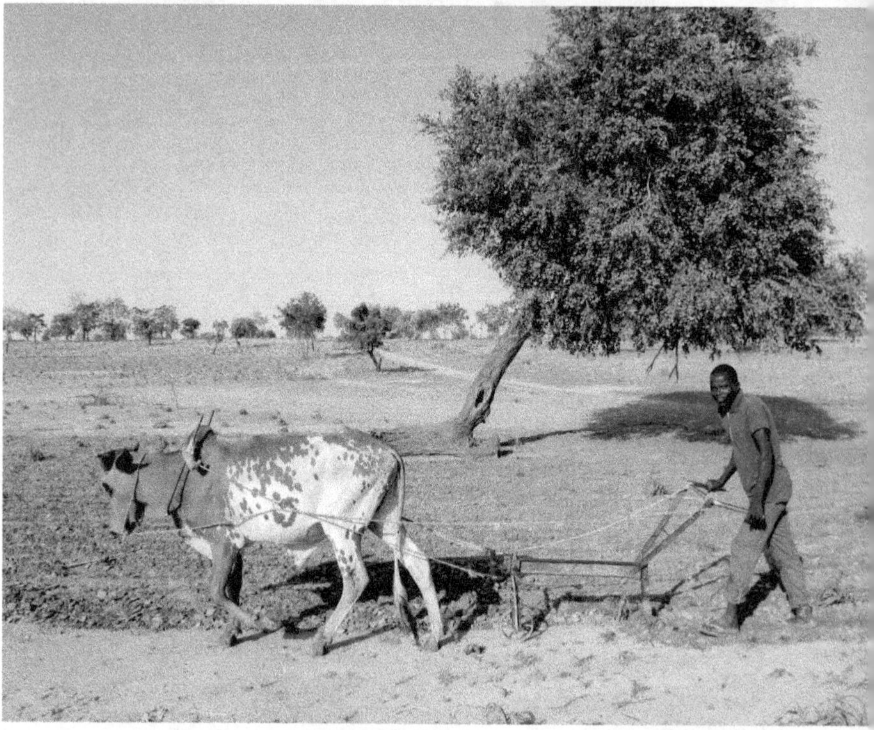

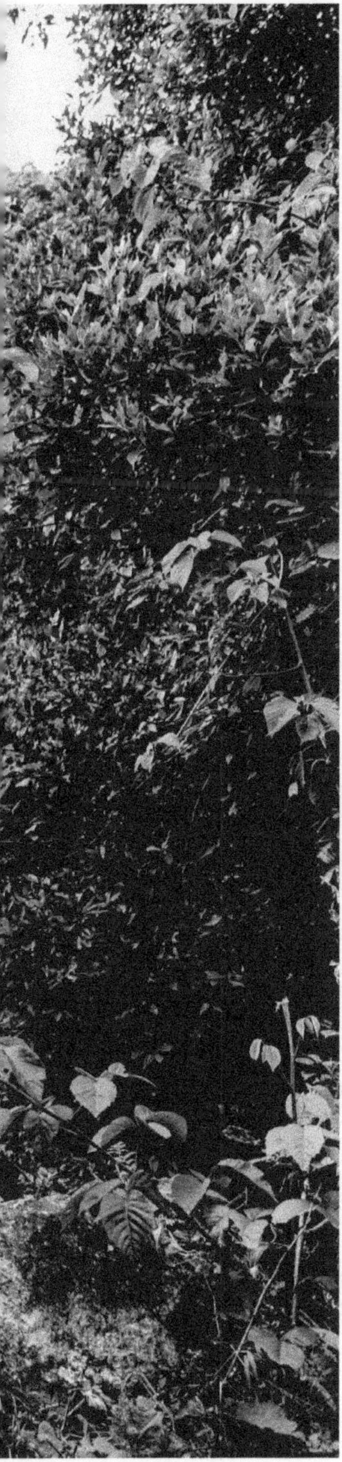

P. 40f. | **Back to nature:** Outside Waye Kaye village in the Maradi region, the farmers keep their fields trim; one farmer ploughs his fields with an ox, just like the old days. A trader loads up his old delivery vehicle with peanut hay which makes good cattle fodder (overleaf).

P. 42f. | Ethiopian Sodo is now transformed into Heidi Land: with picture-book scenes of forests, mountain pastures and bushland.

And finally, the water flows again. In the restored landscape, the groundwater level is rising and replenishes the wells—like here in Sarkin Hatsi village in the Nigerien Maradi region.

below right | In Sodo, Ethiopia, following the FMNR project phase, twelve springs, which had previously dried up, began to flow again.

Discovering the Underground Forest

Tony Rinaudo

I felt a strange mix of joy and foreboding while sitting in the plane heading eastbound from Niger's capital Niamey to the city and district of Maradi in West Africa. 18 years after leaving Maradi—where I had lived with my family for almost two decades—this visit in June 2017 was a homecoming for me. I felt joy that I would be seeing old friends, yet foreboding because success didn't come easily then. The ghosts of old battle foes seemed to rattle their chains of self-doubt at me. Would Maradi look any different to when I had lived there? Would people still practise Farmer Managed Natural Regeneration (FMNR), the farming method that we had developed there? When I had first arrived in Niger in 1980, I was 23 years old and fresh out of university. I was naïve but full of youthful enthusiasm and vigour. There was so much to learn from and about the people here in Maradi, their language, culture and history before even thinking of trees.

We promoted many things during my time in Niger such as energy-saving cooking stoves, tree planting including edible seeded acacias, cassava cultivation, small gardens, indigenous ground cover species, pit latrines, mulching, zai pits, composting and FMNR. Of these, FMNR is the only activity which has spread and continues to be practised routinely until today.

During my visit two things stood out for me. It was deeply satisfying to see how, 34 years after introducing the concept, farmers still actively managed the naturally occurring trees on their once barren land and do so without any external incentives. This knowledge, along with seeing the joy, pride and dignity worn on people's faces was reward enough for the 18 years of considerable struggle and pain involved in birthing an FMNR movement. This concept had indeed become a normal part of farming practice and daily life. FMNR was also about much more than having nice feelings about trees. It is essential to have trees in the landscape and fundamental for achieving food security and economic development.

Through the selection and management of indigenous trees, soil fertility is improved, high temperatures and wind speeds are reduced, more moisture is retained and made available to plants, so effectively reducing the impact of drought; more fodder is produced and hence livestock production is increased. In addition, the trees act as an insurance policy because they can be drawn on when disaster strikes, as it does regularly. In times of drought when all crops fail you can harvest a tree, or part of it to sell for cash to buy food. FMNR also acts as a stepping stone for further development. For example, as indigenous flowering trees return, lucrative beekeeping becomes possible. Certain regenerated indigenous tree species such as the Jujube tree, or *Ziziphus mauritiana,* can be top grafted with improved cultivars commonly named "Apple of the Sahel", greatly increasing the price received for the superior fruit in the market. When I lived in Niger I did not have time to fully develop this value-adding aspect of FMNR and so it was deeply satisfying to see that World Vision staff were now building on the foundation laid by introducing beekeeping and grafting material. I came away from Niger with a deep sense of joy that God had used me to make a difference. The joy on people's faces has stayed with me, while the jangling noise of the chains of doubt has been silenced.

The Beginnings

I grew up in the beautiful Ovens Valley in Australia. Here in my home district and on a global scale, I observed first-hand the disregard for and destruction of the environment in the name of progress, and I followed it globally on television and through reading. I saw that children, just like me who through no fault of their own happened to be born on the other side of the world, were going to bed hungry. My reaction was to feel angry and as a child, powerless. I remember praying a child's prayer to be used somewhere, somehow to make a difference.

An ordinary event was to provide fertile ground for an idea to germinate and begin to grow. I often went with my dad when he visited farms, usually to repair machinery. One day he dropped in on a farmer who had a large pile of second-hand books dumped on the floor in the middle of his tobacco shed. I flipped through a few books and picked up two of interest: "I Planted Trees" and "Sahara Conquest" by Richard St.Barbe Baker. He was an international campaigner from Hampshire in the United Kingdom and fought for the preservation of pristine forests and for the sustainable management and utilization of trees. I read his books cover to cover and was both comforted that there were adults who cared enough to take action, and felt challenged by the enormity and seriousness of the problem. Deforestation was not an inevitable consequence of progress. By going on the front foot something could be done to combat the destruction.

"We had better be without gold than without timber," Baker wrote in "I Planted Trees". "Wood is necessary to civilized life, and therefore it is a basis of civilization. The greatest value of trees is probably their beneficent effect upon life, health, climate, soil, rainfall and streams. Trees beautify the country, provide shade for humans and stock, shelter crops from wind and storm and retain the water in the soil at a level at which it can be used by man. The neglect of forestry in the past has accounted for the deserts that exist, because of the fact that when the tree covering disappears from the earth, the water-level sinks ... When the forests go, the waters go, the fish and game go, crops go, herds and flocks go, fertility departs. Then the age-old phantoms appear stealthily, one after another—flood, drought, fire, famine, pestilence."

With those powerful words in my mind I later went on to study agriculture and while at university I met my wife to be, Liz Fearon. We shared a common sense of calling. After graduation we were married, completed a Bible and Missions course and were accepted for service by the international Christian organization "Serving in Mission" (SIM). SIM is an evangelical, interdenominational mission organization established in 1893 and it works in over 70 countries. We were assigned to Niger Republic, West Africa.

When we arrived in Maradi in 1980 we lived on the outskirts of the city at a property set up as a preparatory Bible and Farm School. We had a generator, which we ran for four hours during the evening for lights, fans and to pump water from a well. My enduring memory of those days was our need to wet the sheets several times before bedtime to cool down the foam mattress sufficiently to be able to sleep. I was shocked by the extreme degree of environmental degradation and I wondered if I, fresh out of university and with no experience, would be able to make any difference at all. Much of the woody vegetation that had been there only 20 or even ten years before my arrival was gone, mostly cut down by farmers. During a series of droughts, out of desperation, people would fell even the last trees—to sell the wood to buy food and meet basic needs. Statistically, an average of only four trees were left per hectare.

We think today that depending on the species regenerated and how farmers manage them, farmland can comfortably support around 100 trees per hectare and still realize a yield increase from annual crops.

At Niger's independence in 1960 the population of the former French colony was under 3.4 million. When I arrived in 1980, the population hadn't quite reached 6 million and by 1984 it was 6.72 million. The cities were growing rapidly and with them the demand for firewood. Maradi's population more than doubled in the ten years after 1977, from 45,000 to 110,000 inhabitants. People in the countryside were poor with few means of earning income, so where trees were still relatively plentiful they were cut down to earn money. The rural population grew as well and the cycles for slash and burn agriculture shortened (this is the fallow period before returning to cultivate abandoned land). It reached a point where no land was being fallowed or only land that had become so exhausted that under the low- or no input agricultural system, it was not worth cultivating.

Deforestation is a precursor of land degradation and desertification. It is estimated that 74% of rangelands and 61% of rain-fed croplands in Africa's drier regions are damaged by moderate to very severe desertification. It occurs on all continents except Antarctica and affects the livelihoods of millions of people, including a large proportion of the poor in drylands. Those drylands occupy 41% of Earth's land area and are home to more than 2 billion people—a third of the human population in the year 2000. They include all terrestrial regions where water scarcity limits the production of crops, forage, wood and other ecosystem provisioning services. Land degradation has a direct impact on predisposition to drought, flood, landslides, pest and disease outbreak.

Desertification also affects global climate change through soil and vegetation losses. Dryland soils contain over a quarter of all organic carbon stores in the world as well as nearly all the inorganic carbon. It is estimated that 300 million tonnes of carbon are lost to the atmosphere from drylands as a result of desertification each year—about 4% of the total global emissions from all sources combined. Deforestation directly and negatively impacts the lives of millions of people. By contrast, reforestation can be a powerful tool to positively impact the most vulnerable people in the world, improving microclimatic conditions, soil fertility, reducing incidence and severity of flood and the impact of drought, increasing food security and water availability and providing a platform for greater resilience to disasters, economic development and diversification of income streams.

The Scarred Reality

After my arrival in Niger I asked myself many times how huge parts of Niger could have been devastated to such an extent. Today, I know that there are many reasons for this. Most farmers in Niger viewed trees on farmland as 'weeds' which needed to be eliminated because they compete with food crops for nutrition. Trees were also seen to attract grain-eating birds—something that no farmer, let alone one living on the edge of hunger, wants to see. Over recent decades some farmers could also afford to buy ox-drawn ploughs: in this case, it was thought better to remove all obstacles such as trees and tree stumps so that the oxen could move unhindered. Before colonial times and—for the majority of poor farmers—also during colonial rule, the people in Niger had cultivated by hand with a hoe.

In addition, colonialists brought the concept of monoculture to Africa. If you want to produce large quantities efficiently you needed to provide ideal conditions for the crop of choice. The crop of choice required by the colonial administration was peanuts and Maradi had become a major production and processing centre. A big oil factory remains to this day, but it stands idle for most of the year. To boost peanut production there were strong extension programmes promoting cultivation with donkey and ox-drawn ploughs and the use of peanut planting machines. Farmers were told that 'modern farmers' cleared trees and stumps from their land to aid cultivation and to increase peanut yields. A farmer in Senegal's peanut basin told me that he remembers clearly the day in the same era that his life changed forever. There was a meeting in the village square and an extension agent was demonstrating planters and ploughs which were being provided on credit. From that day, it was his job and that of the other village boys to clear the land and remove stumps and roots from the field. In the 1970s, the Maradi Productivity Project did the same thing thanks to an intense campaign to modernize agriculture, which involved removal of trees. On the one hand, there was a kind of shaming for those not practising modern agriculture i.e. clearing trees and use of animal traction equipment. And on the other hand, there was an almost irresistible credit offer for very poor farmers who saw this as a way out of poverty.

The combined effect of these attitudes and practices was the almost total destruction of trees and shrubs in the agricultural zone of Niger between the 1950s and 1980s. And this destruction had devastating consequences. Deforestation worsened the adverse effects of recurring drought, strong winds, high temperatures, infertile soils and pests and diseases on crops and livestock. Combined with rapid population growth and poverty these problems contributed to chronic hunger and periodic acute famine. The severe famine of the mid-1970s fuelled a global response and stopping desertification became a top donor, governmental and NGO priority.

Upon arrival in Niger I inherited a small reforestation project which wasn't having much impact. The project involved raising seedlings grown either in a central nursery or in village nurseries, and working with communities to select an area and plant and protect the trees. But usually the trees we planted died because of neglect, animals, drought, sand storms or termites. However, the indifference and even open hostility of many people to the idea of reforestation was a bigger cause of failure, and was very discouraging besides. It seemed incredible (to me at least) that some people actively opposed tree planting. Some thought that we were putting ourselves above God by planting trees—"it was God's work, and if He wanted trees, He would plant them!" Others thought that having trees on their land would just bring disputes—either with the authorities, or with people caught stealing them. In fact, the lack of private tree ownership and the lack of laws and enforcement mechanisms to discourage theft gave scant incentive for anybody to bother with tree growing at all. Additionally, it was generally accepted as 'common knowledge' that trees could not give a return to their owner in his lifetime because they grew too slowly, and that competition and shading from trees lowered crop yields. The problem with common knowledge is that even if it is wrong, or, at least, not correct in all circumstances, it is usually held strongly enough to prevent entertaining any ideas that challenge it.

Even so, I read widely, consulted and experimented with tree planting. I cajoled villagers and I rolled up my sleeves and worked with them. At times, I even used the blunt tool of incentives to try to get people to grow trees for long enough to see the benefits for themselves and continue the practice without me. Incentives are a poor substitute for walking alongside people on a journey of learning and discovery and adoption of new ideas based on knowledge and understanding. Despite all my efforts nothing worked in a cost-effective, sustainable way. In fact, to many I was the 'mad white farmer' and my ideas were just silly. The founder of IBM, Charles Ranlett Flint was once asked how to increase success in business. His response was to double your failure rate. The success story of FMNR follows many failed attempts to reverse deforestation in Niger.

Despite government and NGOs in Niger investing millions of US-dollars and thousands of hours' labour, there was little overall impact. Conventional approaches to reforestation faced insurmountable problems and they are expensive and labour intensive. Even in the nursery where you think you have control, goats, frogs, locusts, termites and birds regularly destroyed seedlings. In this barren landscape, these oases of green became a magnet attracting hungry creatures from far and wide. Once planted out, drought, sand blasting, pests, competition from weeds and destruction by people and animals negated efforts. Low levels of community ownership and the lack of individual or village level replicability meant that no spontaneous, indigenous revegetation movement arose out of these intense efforts. Meanwhile, established indigenous trees continued to disappear at an alarming rate. National forestry laws were ineffective because they took tree ownership and responsibility for care of trees out of the hands of the people and put it in the hands of an under-resourced government.

In some African countries deforestation rates exceed planting rates by 3,000%. In Niger, despite millions of US-dollars spent on nurseries and planting, weeding, fencing and guarding seedlings, few projects made any lasting impression. It is estimated that some 60 million trees were planted in a twelve-year period and less than 20% survived. Even though ineffective and uneconomic, reforestation through conventional tree planting seemed to be the only way to address desertification at the time. Despite predictable failure, the same approach was repeated year after year. The actors, including myself initially did what we thought was best. We failed to test our assumptions. In a personal account of living through the American dust bowl experience one veteran said: "We kept thinking that tomorrow things would change. Sure, you kept doing what you were doing, we thought that maybe there were things that you could do that would make things a bit better than the way they are. You didn't try something different but you just tried it harder, the same thing that didn't work." To a very large degree, we were all doing the same thing year after year, but doing it harder, all the while making no significant difference.

The Discovery

After two and a half years of mounting frustration I was ready to give up. At one of my lowest points, I was driving to the villages with a trailer load of seedlings. The hopelessness of it all weighed heavily on me. I stopped to reduce the air pressure in the tyres to help the vehicle travel more easily over the loose sand. While stopped I looked over the barren landscape. North, South, East, West: as far as I could see there were empty, windswept plains almost completely devoid of trees. I realized that it would not matter if I had a multimillion-dollar budget, many years to do the work and hundreds of staff—using the methods I was currently using would never make a significant or lasting impact. It was hopeless and I was on the verge of going home.

Even so, I still felt I was meant to be in Niger. Faith has always played a big role in my decision making, and at that low point I reached out again for help. In short, I asked God to forgive us for destroying the gift of his beautiful creation, knowing that much of the suffering and hunger people were experiencing was directly related to environmental degradation, and I asked God to open my eyes and to show me what to do.

On this day, one of the common small 'bushes' growing in the field caught my eye. I had 'seen' these bushes many times before but had never registered their significance. Today, I walked over to take a closer look. On seeing the leaves, I realized that this was not a bush at all—it was a tree, which had been cut down, and it was re-sprouting from the stump. In that instant, everything changed. I somehow knew that this was the solution I had been looking for—and it had been at my feet the whole time! There were millions of similar bushes belying the fact that a vast underground forest existed just beneath the surface of that seemingly barren landscape. Each year, re-sprouting stems would grow to about one metre in height—and then, in preparation for sowing the crops, farmers would slash that growth and either burn the stems and branches and leaves for ash to fertilize the soil—or take the stems and branches home for fuel wood. For as long as this regular slashing and burning continued, the 'bushes' would never regrow into full-sized trees, and the 'forest' would remain hidden underground.

When a tree is felled, for most species, much of the root mass remains alive and the tree has the capacity to regrow rapidly from the stump due to its access to soil moisture and nutrients and its large store of starch in the roots. Felled trees constitute 'underground' forests, because we do not see them and tend to discount the potential of the seemingly insignificant shoots that sprout from stumps. By selecting and pruning superior stems and by culling surplus stems, one achieves rapid growth with superior form.

In 'discovering' this underground forest, the battle lines were immediately redrawn. Reforestation was no longer a question of having the right technology or enough budget, staff or time. It was not even about fighting the Sahara Desert, or goats or drought. The battle was now about challenging deeply held beliefs, attitudes and practices and convincing people that it would be in their best interest to allow at least some of these 'bushes' to become trees again. I realized that if it was people who had reduced the forest to a barren landscape, it would require people to restore it—and false beliefs, attitudes and practices would need to be challenged with truth, love and perseverance.

From time to time I reflect on that revelation. Why hadn't I 'seen' the bushes for what they were earlier? Why had much smarter, more highly qualified and better paid people than me also missed seeing them? I now believe that if your assumptions about a problem are wrong at the outset of a venture, then everything you do to solve the problem will be off the mark, and you are in danger of being blind to solutions that are literally at your feet. I, like all those who'd gone before me, thought that the trees had been completely removed and that tree planting was the only way to restore them. I had heard and also assumed from my short observations that indigenous trees were slow growing and they were inferior in quality to exotic species. And I assumed that the Sahara Desert was moving south.

In fact, there was no need to plant trees—they were already there in their millions, but hidden in the 'underground forest' of buried tree stumps, roots and seeds. Indigenous trees, especially when growing from a mature stump, can grow very quickly and unlike many exotics, they are adapted to local conditions. While it was true that most indigenous trees in Niger would not produce high-value millable timber, they are extremely useful for fuel, traditional construction, fodder, medicine, dyes, rope, fertilizer, shade and reducing wind speeds and high temperatures, building soil fertility and more. As it turned out, it was not the Sahara Desert that we were fighting, but people's beliefs, attitudes and practices towards land and vegetation management. Having a correct set of assumptions makes all the difference to how you will tackle the problem and to your chances of success.

FMNR is a cheap and rapid method of revegetation which can be applied over large areas of land and can be adapted to a range of land use systems. It is simple and can be adapted to each individual farmer's unique requirements. FMNR provides multiple benefits to people, livestock, crops and the environment. Through managing natural regeneration, farmers, pastoralists and forest-dependent communities can control their own resources without dependence on externally funded projects or the need to buy expensive inputs: seed, fertilizers and nursery supplies. Its beauty lies in its simplicity and accessibility to even the poorest—and once it has been accepted, it takes on a life of its own, spreading from farmer to farmer, by word of mouth.

The method is not actually new; it is simply a form of coppicing and pollarding, which has a history of over 1,000 years in Europe and examples can be found in various parts of the world. It was new, however, to many contemporary farmers in Niger who since colonization viewed trees on farmland as 'weeds' which needed to be eliminated. For my part, even though growing up in Australia, I had seen Eucalyptus trees re-sprout after being cut, I did not make the connection between that knowledge and what I believed at the time were useless bushes on farmland. I was not looking for a solution in the ground. I was looking for a solution from overseas experience and species. I was stuck on a tram track of thought that assumed that there were no trees left in the fields and the only solution would involve some permutation of raising seedlings in a nursery.

Never Waste a Good Crisis

The discovery of the 'underground forest' didn't take Niger by storm. In fact, acceptance of FMNR was slow at first. The paradigm of a good farmer being a 'clean' farmer, one who clears trees from his land, was deeply ingrained, and nobody in that culture wanted to be seen questioning or going against accepted wisdom. I conducted village meetings and had discussions with village chiefs, but in the beginning, I could only convince around 12 farmers in as many villages to at least try FMNR on a small corner of their land. They were the 'early adopters' in their communities who had already hardened themselves against criticism, or some may have been people who felt financially secure enough to take a risk. They became the butt of many jokes and were ridiculed for being so foolish as to leave trees on their crop land. As the trees started to grow and FMNR was showing promise, their trees were often cut and stolen by others. Wood was a scarce and valuable commodity, and traditionally, trees were a gift of God for all to exploit. No doubt, some were destroyed out of jealousy, or spite and even fear of breaking with tradition.

Ironically, a devastating drought and severe famine in the mid-1980s helped.

The harsh reality of famine was sharpening people's thinking on the importance of trees. Perhaps for the first time they began to associate the increasing frequency and severity of droughts with the loss of trees. In response to the famine, our team mounted a Food for Work Programme through which we introduced the concept of FMNR to around 70,000 people in almost 100 villages, resulting in FMNR being practised on about 12,500 hectares. The struggle to obtain official permission to distribute food, funds and even grain is a story on its own but we were deeply moved by the generosity of hundreds of people from around the world who gave liberally to SIM's relief appeal. Between these gifts enabling us to purchase grain and smaller grants of food aid by the World Food Programme and USAID we were able to distribute 1,800 tonnes of grain over the critical food shortage period preceding the next harvest.

We assembled a team with the twofold goal of feeding people while introducing FMNR at scale. The Food for Work Programme gave an opportunity to introduce our new strategy to a critical mass of people for an extended period so that they could experience the benefits for themselves. Many were surprised that their crops grew better amongst the trees. All benefited from having a small amount of fuel wood as a product of pruning and thinning the regrowth. With the protective umbrella of the Food for Work Programme and the full support of village and district chiefs as well as the forestry service, the stigma of being different disappeared and theft of trees was kept to a minimum.

I managed a team of around ten salaried local staff and varying numbers of part-time FMNR champions who lived in the villages and were expected to practise and demonstrate what they taught others on their own land first. Several missionaries working on various aspects of the project including administration, community health and agriculture also supported the project. Local staff were the front-line troops of the movement. Their hardships are unheralded—they drank the same well water and ate the same food as the villagers and sometimes suffered from the same illnesses as the people they served. They lived in grass huts and mud brick houses without electricity and endured both high and low temperatures and sandstorms without complaining. They were often the butt of jokes, regularly ignored and sometimes targeted with physical or emotional harm or deliberate loss or damage of their property. Importantly, they persevered no matter what, they won confidence and in time influenced a whole generation of farmers. Initially, the project was jointly managed by myself and a representative of SIM's partner organization, the Evangelical Church of Niger (EERN). I greatly benefited from the wisdom, example and social standing of my EERN colleague, Pasteur Cherif Yacouba, in those early years.

Working with the local community our team started selecting, pruning and managing these 'bushes' creating a natural agroforestry system, rather than a tree-planting one. One that uses what is already in the ground and is propelled by a process owned and driven by farmers and communities themselves. In time, a re-greening FMNR movement, involving the systematic regeneration and management of farmer-selected, naturally occurring trees and shrubs from stumps, roots and seeds emerged and began to spread across Niger. Each year, live tree stumps sprout multiple shoots. In practising FMNR the farmer selects the stumps she or he wants to leave and decides how many shoots are wanted per stump. Excess shoots are then cut and side branches trimmed to half way up the stems. A good farmer will return regularly to do a touch up pruning to remove suckers and new branches. There is no set system or hard and fast rules. Farmers are given guidelines but are free to choose which species they manage, the number of shoots per stump and the number of stumps per hectare that they leave, and the time span between subsequent pruning and harvest of stems and the method of pruning.

There is a technical side to reforestation, whether through methods such as tree planting, involving species selection, seed sourcing, raising seedlings in a nursery, site selection and preparation, fencing, guarding out, maintenance or FMNR, which involves selection, pruning and management of growth from stumps, roots and seed. But there is also a social side to it. Land needing reforestation is often inhabited or at least used by people. In such settings, it is very important to engage all stakeholders—for example, sedentary farmers and nomadic herders who pass through only for a few months of the year, men, women and children, government representatives including forestry and department of agriculture agents, merchants and staff of other NGOs, traditional chiefs and religious leaders. Great effort is required to ensure that they understand and are not only in agreement but want the land reforested, building their capacity and equipping and empowering them to make decisions and enabling them to benefit from their efforts. These activities are critical elements in an FMNR project. The success of FMNR lies in working with communities to build an enabling environment that allows them to develop their capabilities in organization, networking, dealing with authorities and creating governance systems. Today individuals and communities, which had lost hope and had felt like helpless victims of poverty and climate change, are being empowered to address their situation. FMNR does not create dependency and it is bottom up, putting individuals and communities firmly in the decision-making seat. In a very real sense, FMNR is restoring hope and giving people back their dignity and sense of belonging.

And lastly, there is also a policy dimension. Many countries have devised well-meaning laws to protect trees, making them the property of the government. There is certainly a place for this, but this policy has largely failed, particularly in low income countries, because it has not taken into account the desperate needs of millions of smallholder farmers and their families who depend on the natural resource base, including trees, for their livelihoods. These policies have taken responsibility for sustainable management of trees and legal benefit from the hands of people living off the natural resource base and awarding it to local or national authorities which are sometimes corrupt, but often simply too under-resourced to be able to police the whole landscape effectively.

The government of Niger automatically adopted the French forestry code put in place by the colonists. All naturally occurring trees were therefore the property of the state, ostensibly to protect them. Thus, there was no incentive for farmers to look after the trees on their own land and much of the destruction of that era was linked to this well-meaning but misguided policy. After discussions with the head of the Maradi district Forestry Department, verbal permission was given to try a different approach. Our project staff began giving assurances that if farmers cared for the trees on their land they would be allowed to harvest them and benefit without fear of being fined. Farmers who were still obliged to pay a low permit fee began to sell fuel wood at local markets without undue hassle. And as the perception of trees on farms switched from trees being a liability and a weed to becoming a cash crop in their own right, farmers became highly motivated to manage trees. Over time, locally agreed codes and rules with support from village and district chiefs were sometimes established, greatly facilitating the spread of FMNR. In reality, in Niger FMNR spread on the strength of a perception that they now owned the trees! However, tree ownership and user right laws did not change officially until decades later.

Another hurdle for our work turned out to be the rather artificial division of the disciplines of forestry and agriculture. In reality, there is no hard and fast cut-off point where pure agriculture and pure forestry begin or end: they are two components of a continuum. These constructs create their own methodologies, idealized outcomes and bureaucracies. At one extreme, agriculture cannot entertain the presence of trees on cultivated land and at the other, forest departments set up primarily for the protection of trees look unfavourably on the harvesting of trees. Historically in Niger, foresters have legal jurisdiction over trees on agricultural land, and following national policies, they had been tasked to protect them and prevent their disappearance. Agriculturalists on the other hand have generally not seen trees on agricultural land as being within their portfolio, and they have had no incentive to promote their protection.

The Germination of a Movement

At the end of the famine and our Food for Work Programme the result of our efforts was rather disappointing. Over two thirds of the approximately half a million trees protected that year were chopped down once the programme ended at the next grain harvest in October 1985. This was partly because old habits die hard, but also because it is hard for poor people to wait for a tree to grow when they can make quick money today selling firewood. Many harvested their trees in order to avoid having them stolen. And others still simply didn't believe that trees and crops were compatible. As it soon turned out, the seed of a movement had germinated nevertheless. There were enough farmers now who were convinced of the benefits of FMNR who did not cut down their regenerating trees and who could sway public opinion. From this critical mass of early adopters, an FMNR movement emerged and began to spread. Gradually more and more farmers started protecting trees and word spread from farmer to farmer until it became a standard practice.

From 1985 to 1999 we adopted a strategy of promoting FMNR locally, nationally and even internationally when the opportunity presented itself. Exchange visits and training days were organized for various NGOs, government foresters, Peace Corps Volunteers as well as farmer- and civil society groups from across Niger. We encouraged them to come and spend time in our villages and learn from our FMNR practitioners. Additionally, our project staff and farmers were sent to numerous locations across Niger to provide training. The importance of these exchanges should not be underestimated. If it were not for the 1984 famine and subsequent Food for Work Programme, which mobilized a whole district, there may well have been no FMNR scale-up story today. Peer group pressure can force people to even not do things which they know would benefit them. The mindset may be 'better to do without than to be ostracized'. It may be that the unity of the community is cherished because it has been a powerful means of ensuring cohesion and survival in a harsh environment. Beyond Maradi, my theory is that taking people out of their immediate village setting and exposing them to other settings where FMNR was 'normalized' liberated some to be bold and introduce change at home.

While we were actively promoting FMNR, in some places farmers were independently drawing their own conclusions about the importance of trees and were spontaneously developing their own approaches to tree regeneration. For example, in the Zinder Department, farmers have almost exclusively practised FMNR with *Faidherbia albida,* a fertilizer and fodder tree which is very compatible with Nigerien agro-pastoral systems. In the Maradi area, farmers favoured *Philostigma reticulatum* and *Guiera senegalensis* which grow faster than *F. albida,* have harder wood and no thorns. In the Aguie sub-district farmers coming back from work in Nigeria after the rains had already started had no time to clear their land of emerging trees like their neighbours. Because of the strong winds, they were surprised to discover that their late sown crops performed better than their neighbours' crops. And so, in this district, pruning and thinning of regrowth occurred in the rainy season, not before the rains as was the case in Maradi.

I left Niger in 1999, only aware of the transformation in the State of Maradi where I'd worked. I did not know the extent of the spread of FMNR in Niger until I met the Dutch Human Geographer, Chris Reij in 2004. By drawing on the work of Gray Tappan from the US Geological Survey, which uses satellite imagery, Chris and Gray estimated that FMNR was being practised on over 5,000,000 hectares of land in Niger alone. Reij went onto describe the spread of FMNR as one of the biggest positive environmental changes in the Sahel and perhaps all of Africa. A new study by Gray in 2016 now estimates that FMNR is being practised on 6,000,000 hectares across Niger.

This is a significant achievement by the people of Niger. That this happened in one of the world's poorest countries—in a physically and socially hostile environment with little investment in the forestry sector by either the government or NGOs—makes it doubly significant to countries facing similar problems. The Niger example begs the question: if such rapid and low cost reforestation is possible under such difficult conditions, what might be possible elsewhere? Indeed, the Niger story today is providing a beacon of light and hope to the earth's degraded landscapes.

Mixed Feelings

After 18 years living and working in Niger, it was time to return to Australia. On the one hand, it was an easy decision. There were family needs, I was exhausted from famine relief activities and it was time to break unhealthy dependency that ensued due to my involvement in relief. I had been influenced by Roland Bunch, author of "Two Ears of Corn, A Guide to People-Centred Agricultural Improvement", who wrote: "If what you do does not last, you have done nothing at all." And so, it was time to see if FMNR would continue to be practised even if I was not there. By this time people were aware of the benefits, and I believed that my staying longer would not make any difference to adoption.

On the other hand, it was very difficult to leave the people I had come to know and love, and the work which I had dedicated a large part of my life to. I wondered what I could do back home that was as fulfilling as this. While it had been 'right' to take a leap of faith and move my family to Niger in my youth, the prospect of finding meaningful work in Australia seemed dim and I was worried. Relief came when a friend sent me a clipping of an advertisement for a position with World Vision Australia. I immediately felt that this was a role that I could whole heartedly throw my energy into from Australia and it would give an unprecedented opportunity to apply the hard lessons learnt in Niger on a very large canvas.

I joined World Vision Australia in 1999 as a programme officer for their projects in Kenya and Ethiopia. While I oversaw the full range of schemes—Water and Sanitation for Health, Gender, Child Sponsorship, Maternal and Child Health, Agriculture—I could see how the sustainability of all the sectors that World Vision was implementing depended on having a healthy, functioning environment. As had been the case in Niger, Kenya and Ethiopia had lost much of their original forest cover. Both countries faced serious land degradation issues and were vulnerable to both drought and flood as a consequence. For the most part, people relied on annual rain-fed grain crops in an often unreliable climate, too often resulting in crop failure, hunger and in severe cases, famine. In both countries, rural people depended heavily on dwindling tree reserves for their supply of fuel wood, construction timber and non-timber forest products. Having witnessed the power of FMNR in Niger to bring about greater resilience to drought, I had a burning desire to help people elsewhere restore their land so that they could live dignified, even abundant lives. So, I sought opportunities to introduce FMNR to the World Vision partnership.

Generating a Movement

I did not want to simply initiate FMNR projects in various countries. Projects have defined start and end dates, set geographical foci, calculated outcomes and fixed budgets. As likely as not, once the last dollar is spent, the work stops. As far as possible, I wanted to replicate what happened in Niger. Unlike projects, social movements do not have clearly defined start and end dates. There is spontaneity about them and the element of surprise. Movements are not limited to geographical boundaries, their outcomes can be way above and beyond expectations, and outputs are not necessarily proportional to budget size. As likely as not, once the last dollar is spent, the work continues to spread.

Social movements by their very nature cannot be orchestrated. We can implement key elements which we think will contribute towards creating a movement, but because movements depend on the actions of individuals and circumstances, we cannot predict when, or how a movement will occur. 1984 in Niger was the right time and place for the emergence of a movement. The severe famine of 1984 capped a series of hit and miss years in which farming practices were regularly failing to meet people's basic needs. Each year, people lived in great uncertainty over growing sufficient food to see them through till the next harvest. In fact, it was more certain not to grow enough food than vice versa. Poverty was increasing. Soil fertility was depleted. The lack of tree cover forced farmers to replant their seed six or more times in very windy years. Farmers were playing Russian roulette by expanding cultivation northward into an even less favourable climatic zone where likelihood of crop failure was even greater. Crossing the desert in search of work was hazardous. Going South to Nigeria came with hardships and uncertainties of its own. When FMNR was thrown into this brew of undesirable choices—it was embraced. I believe this is because FMNR met several felt needs simultaneously, including increasing the certainty of harvesting a grain crop, higher crop yields, fuel wood, fodder, increased soil fertility and protection from strong winds—and all this starts within the first growing season and costs nothing. And they embraced it because it is a 'no regrets' technology. That is, there is little risk, little to lose through its application, but potentially very much to gain. For people left with few choices in life, this was one change that was easy to embrace. In addition though, in Maradi Department at least, there was now comfort in numbers. The 1984 Food for Work Programme created a critical mass of farmers practising FMNR. This had the effect of decreasing negative peer group pressure to conform to the normal practice of clearing trees from farms.

How does one create a successful FMNR movement in new settings with different circumstances? There is no single answer to this question. But we draw from a suite of interventions trying to best match the selection to the specific country situation. We create awareness through meetings, workshops, conferences and media. We create pilot areas to demonstrate the impact. We train and equip FMNR champions and facilitate exchange visits because we see farmers themselves as the premier agents of change and influence. We equip people with knowledge and skill on how to tackle obstacles to FMNR uptake. We engage all stakeholders and especially leaders (government, traditional and religious authorities, youth, women, marginalized groups) and endeavour to firstly create awareness of the link between deforestation and impoverishment, and secondly to empower them to act. We walk alongside for a period—visiting, learning together, coaching, correcting, encouraging and supporting especially where there is conflict and danger of reversals. This is time consuming. It requires patience and above all, it requires empathy. Nobody cares about how much you know until they know how much you care. We encourage the formation of appropriate FMNR groups for solidarity and mutual support. Often there is a need for advocacy for laws to be changed so that farmers will have the necessary assurance that if they practice FMNR, they will benefit. We look for market linkages to generate economic sustainability and we facilitate value adding through introducing or scaling up activities such as beekeeping and grafting of superior fruit cultivars onto wild regenerated trees. Having mixed all the known key ingredients into the recipe—we persevere, and we wait. One year? Two years? Five years? In Niger, there were clear signs of emergence of a movement within 10 years, however we did not know the extent of the movement until twenty years later. Today, by building on the foundation already laid, we are beginning to see signs of emergence of movements in as little as one to five years.

I had a lot to learn not only about creating movements, but about how to move a large organization. I wrote articles, I gave talks and I presented at seminars thinking that knowledge of the magnitude of FMNR's impact and spread in Niger would elicit action. There was interest, but no follow-up. When talking and writing about success is not enough—action is required. Realizing that activities undertaken by World Vision field offices were largely determined by their national office strategy, annual plans and budget allocation, I next turned my attention to designing and obtaining funding for projects with FMNR components in them. I thought that change could only come about when there was a dedicated budget for activities with accountable targets which would be measured and evaluated. There was merit in this approach.

Growing Cabbages in Your Head

World Vision's first project to include promotion of FMNR began in five countries in West Africa. Unfortunately, this project did not have the impact I had hoped for. In hindsight, I do not think I gave adequate support or follow-up. New ideas require time and persistent effort and mentoring to take hold. There were some staff capacity issues in some countries. It was difficult for the programme manager to keep on top of issues across five countries on a limited budget. Consequently, FMNR uptake was not significant and field staff often defaulted to spending more time promoting more readily accepted interventions. Even so, this pilot project generated some interest in several of the countries and provided important lessons which contributed to the success of subsequent FMNR projects in the region. Importantly, from a World Vision 'child-focused' perspective, a 2011 review put FMNR in terms that World Vision understood and could respond to. The review concluded: "FMNR represents one of the rare projects that could be designed to have the broadest coverage of all children in the Area Programmes in terms of coverage of tangible benefits and its potential for involving children in the design, implementation, monitoring and evaluation of activities. No other Area Programme component offers such holistic opportunities for children as FMNR does. No cultural barriers prevent open dialogue between parents and children on FMNR issues. Because women and children already provide 90% of the household agricultural labour FMNR could become a strategic liberating mechanism for children and women and empower them to play their rightful roles towards building a future that is better than the one they would otherwise passively inherit from their parents." In order to move an organization, it's important to speak the language of that organization and to demonstrate how the desired change will help it achieve its goals.

Subsequent FMNR projects in Senegal and Ghana benefited from field staff leadership with technical backstopping from World Vision Australia. This strong, visionary leadership at the field level, with encouragement and technical support has proven to be a key ingredient for successful introduction and adoption of FMNR.

Perhaps surprisingly, in Senegal initially the biggest push back came from World Vision staff themselves. They believed, not without reason, that farmers would never agree to leave trees on their farms. So, the first hurdle was to convince our own staff that, while there will be strong resistance from farmers, the impact of FMNR makes the effort required worthwhile. Staff, and subsequently, whole communities soon responded positively. Over a period of just five years, in Senegal, FMNR spread to 65,000 hectares and tree density rose from a base line of close to zero trees per hectare to over 37 trees per hectare. In Katie Smith's book "The Human Farm. A Tale of Changing Lives and Changing Lands" development agent Eliaz Sanchez says: "You have to see cabbages growing in your head before you can see them growing in the ground." In other words, you must be convinced in your own mind about the value of FMNR before you will practise it. And your own staff must be convinced before they can convince others. We have come to expect resistance to change and we see it as normal. As philosopher Arthur Schopenhauer observed centuries ago: "Every truth passes through three stages before it is recognized. In the first, it is ridiculed. In the second, it is opposed. In the third it is regarded as self-evident."

The root of the matter: What you believe
One of the big hurdles that FMNR regularly faces is beliefs and attitudes about trees and these must be tackled head on. Many farmers believe that trees and crops are incompatible. They believe that if you have trees on your land, they will shade the crops, lowering yields. Farmers also believe that trees will attract grain-eating birds. Many also believe that trees are slow growing and that they will not benefit from their work in their lifetime.

In fact, farmers have a very high degree of control over how much competition trees cause. They can choose which species to leave on their farms—some tree species do indeed suppress crop and pasture growth, but not all. They can choose how many trees they leave on their land, thus controlling tree density. And, they can choose how severely they prune the trees that they leave, so controlling the amount of shade. Tree crop interactions deserve greater research. Even so research findings to date reveal that some tree species under some conditions significantly and positively boost crop yields. Tests conducted by the World Agroforestry Centre over a four-year period in Zambia revealed a two to threefold yield increase by crops under the canopy of *Faidherbia albida* trees. *F. albida* puts a plant-available form of nitrogen fertilizer back into the soil and since it sheds its leaves in the rainy season, it allows adequate light to get through while reducing temperatures. Eleven years of research undertaken by a consortium of scientists in Senegal revealed that without fertilizer addition, *Philostigma reticulatum* shrub plots had approximately two times greater millet yield throughout the duration of this experiment. *P. reticulatum* can draw water from deep in the soil profile and redistribute it at shallow soil layers, making moisture available to annual crop plants. Thus, even in drought years, crops growing close to *P. reticulatum* can perform surprisingly well.

At the time of writing, 34 years after introducing the FMNR concept to Niger and after realizing an expansion of FMNR to six million hectares, I have never heard of an incident of grain-eating birds destroying crops. This is not proof that there has been none. However, if it were a significant problem, almost certainly farmers, and especially farmers who experience hunger regularly, would not have continued practising FMNR.

Many farmers do not bother growing trees because they believe that they take too long to grow. They have immediate, urgent needs that they see as having precedence for their attention. A surprising thing about FMNR, even in arid and semi-arid conditions, is just how fast trees can grow, especially when growing from a mature tree stump. By year three, FMNR trees in Niger were attaining a height of five or more metres.

The point I am making is that beliefs and attitudes towards trees can make the difference between successful FMNR uptake and failure. Where beliefs and attitudes are not true, they need to be respectfully and patiently challenged with facts. Change agents may not always be able to affect such necessary changes on their own. A wise old farmer once said to me: "Tony, if you tell us something we don't really believe it, because if you are wrong, you will not suffer any consequences for your advice but we will. Even if your staff tell us, we do not believe them. They are paid to give that advice whether it is right or wrong. However, if a farmer tells us something, and we see him doing it himself, we listen because we know that his livelihood depends on it being right." Farmers all over the world look at and learn from what their neighbours are doing. Peer to peer exchange is one of the most powerful ways to change beliefs and attitudes. Accordingly, in our FMNR promotion programmes a lot of weight is given to facilitating exchange visits, establishment of model farms and villages and equipping and empowering farmers themselves to be the main agents of change.

The "Past, Present and Future" Exercise

New projects require careful planning and wide consultation. In 2009, I reviewed a concept note for a tree-planting project in Ghana. The proponents did not know about FMNR. As is common, even though success rates are usually low, tree planting is widely accepted as the industry standard for restoring vegetation. Fortunately, World Vision Ghana accepted my offer to provide training and the Talensi FMNR project was kick-started with a workshop for stakeholders including men and women from the communities, religious and traditional leaders, District Commissioner's representatives, forestry and agriculture departments, the forestry research institute, staff from World Vision in Ghana and Australia and the media. It is important to include all stakeholders, hence the wide range of participants' backgrounds. When you want to make changes to how a shared natural resource base (land, vegetation, water) is used, it is critical to include all users in discussions and decision making. Not to do so is to court failure from the outset.

During the workshop, I ran what I call a "Past, Present, Future" exercise in which I divide the audience into three groups. Group one is asked to give a response to the question: "What was the environment like when you were a child?" Group two is asked: "What is the environment like now?" and group three: "If we continue with business as usual and continue degrading the land, what will the environment be like for our children and grandchildren?"

Group one reported that in their childhood, there were still many wild animals and much bushland close at hand, soils were fertile and harvests generally plentiful. Springs, wells and streams did not dry up and there were fewer pests and diseases. Drought and flood were less common and less severe; there was less dust and winds did not blow their roofs off. Temperatures were cooler.

Group two reported that they had witnessed massive environmental changes in their lifetimes including an increase in wildfires, disappearance of bushland and wildlife, declining soil fertility and crop yields, reduced water availability, increases in insect pests, more variable and severe weather events including increasing severity and frequency of drought and flood, more dust and stronger winds. Consequently, the community was poor, often hungry and many of their children were not in school.

Group three reported that as things deteriorate into the future, they would be forced to leave everything that they know and love and move to the city.

Most people, especially the older generation, already know what they have lost, but may not have articulated it in public before. They are painfully aware of their current difficult circumstances. And they know the consequences of continuing down the path they have started on. Frankly, this exercise is a wake-up call. In Uganda one workshop participant said that life would become "hell-on-earth" if things were left to run their course. In Lesotho, somebody offered that "desperation would push them into cannibalism". This exercise hits a raw nerve. It is a key activity for helping people to draw their own conclusions about the need for change. People can see that there are only two choices: to do nothing and accept an inevitable fate of hunger and poverty for their children, or, to change and act to avert disaster.

For many this exercise sparks a light bulb moment which predisposes participants to want to take action. This, in combination with sharing 'before' and 'after' photos and the Niger FMNR story often convinces people that they are not hopeless victims of climate change and poverty, and that they can create a better future for their children.

There is a wise Senegalese proverb which says: "If you are on a journey and you lose your way, go back to where you started from and you will be able to work out the right direction from there." Most farmers know that they have lost their way and their current way of farming is not meeting their family's needs. While not all traditional farming methods were in harmony with nature, generally there were rotations and recovery (fallow) times which allowed nature to heal itself and there was greater utilization of biodiversity. In recent times, populations have grown and the practice of fallow has been reduced or not practised at all. With modernization, the trend is to remove all trees from farms and to rely on a few, usually annual, staple crops. FMNR offers a way for farmers to get back closer to where farming started, in the forests and on the treed plains, and from there to work out a better direction to take.

Power Analysis

Another significant exercise conducted at the workshop was to do a power analysis. The purpose is to determine who the decision makers are and who influences opinions. Having identified this group, a strategy was then adopted to target opinion leaders first and convince them of the value of FMNR, and then to work with them to influence the whole community. In this case, local government, traditional chiefs and traditional land custodians were identified. Once convinced, these influential groups persuaded their communities to try FMNR in pilot sites.

It is important to identify and pre-empt where opposition might come from. Illegal wood cutters and charcoal makers will fear that their means of survival will be taken from them and so it is natural for them to oppose any perceived move to protect or manage the forest. Nomadic herders in Senegal have had free range grazing rights in the farming zone during the dry season for thousands of years. When they saw FMNR trees growing on this land, they saw it as a ploy by land owners to eventually block their access. Government officials may fear loss of potential revenue from land sale or rent if they sign away user rights to communities. One should never underestimate the potential for strong opposition, even to the point of violence. As a young man, Gebre Michael Gidey was convinced that their village farmlands in Tigray, Ethiopia, were turning to desert because of the unbridled destruction of the forest on the surrounding hills. His self-appointment as protector of the forest was not taken too kindly by those profiting from its destruction. One time he was imprisoned after being falsely accused of spying against the government. He could have died there but for the persistent efforts of his sister. Another time his house was fire bombed at night.

A Burning Issue

Another common obstacle to FMNR in many countries is the use and abuse of fire. In the case of Talensi, Ghana, the common practice of annual bush burning needed to be addressed if the project was going to succeed. In fact, most workshop participants thought it would be impossible to stop fires occurring, variously blaming others and stating that it was the government's responsibility, or that World Vision should "do something about it". Development is both an art and a science. At this juncture, I cajoled the participants into taking responsibility for what was essentially their problem. A plan was devised. Communities nominated 100 youth (young men and women) to form volunteer fire brigades. The local fire authority provided training on how to prevent fire in the first place, and how to extinguish it when it occurs. World Vision provided uniforms and very basic firefighting tools including rakes, jute sacks and buckets. The communities created fire breaks as an extra precaution. As an incentive, the local government offered a significant development grant—such as a school, clinic or water supply—for any community which remained fire free for three years.

Serendipity can play a role also. Following the Ghana workshop, a young chief led his community to pilot FMNR on a hillside within view of the village. One day while having a bucket bath in a traditional 'bathroom' consisting of a grass mat that you can see over, the chief was horrified to see that fire had broken out and was heading towards the trees. Forgetting everything, he grabbed the bucket and ran to put out the fire wearing a towel! Somewhat shocked, at that point it dawned on the community that if the trees were that important to the chief, then they must be important indeed. They saved the emerging forest and a milestone in adoption was passed.

Peace Between Bees and Cattle

No new intervention is painted onto a clean canvas. Every community has a history and sometimes it is not pretty, but again, proper steps need to be taken to avoid derailment of the intervention. Conflict between farmers and herders is common, and can sometimes be deadly. In 2010, some beekeepers in Bugesera, Rwanda, formed a cooperative with the aim of increasing honey production. However, their efforts were frustrated by local cattle herders who grazed their animals in the same area as the hives. Resenting the bees, which often stung the cattle, the herders would allow the cattle to knock over the hives and they painted insecticide on their cattle, which killed the bees.

A World Vision FMNR project was initiated in the same district in 2012. Hearing about the situation, the project facilitator talked to both parties and persuaded them to work together on clearing bush encroachment and regenerating the indigenous trees in the area to produce more fodder for both the bees and the cattle. In order to not disturb the bees, the cattle keepers agreed to keep their cattle out of the area where the bee hives were placed, and to harvest the grass by hand.

This approach to conflict resolution proved to be critical to success. Regeneration of the indigenous trees has increased both the quantity and the variety of flowers available for the bees and increased the amount of grass available for the cattle. The trees also produce herbal medicines which are used for treating both human and cattle ailments. The production of honey has doubled and its quality has improved as the variety of indigenous trees has increased. With increased incomes, the group could buy improved beehives.

Reconciliation between the two groups means that beekeepers have easy access to purchase dairy products and the herders can buy honey whenever they wish. In this and similar cases, FMNR was used as a connector, bringing traditional enemies together to solve common problems with amazing results. In some regions conflict between farmers and herders has been reduced by 70% because, instead of experiencing fierce competition for dwindling resources, where FMNR is practised at scale, 'resource expansion' is being experienced. That is, there is an increase in fodder, fuel wood, food and in some cases, even water. It is significant when competing interests come to the realization that it is in everybody's mutual best interest to restore and sustainably manage the natural resource base.

One way to pre-empt problems is to jointly develop community by-laws from the outset. By-laws outline people's rights and responsibilities with regard to tree management and clearly lay out agreed consequences for infringements. Typically, by-laws will state who has the right to harvest timber, how it will be harvested and for what uses it can be harvested for. Punishment for cutting others' trees and who and how the punishment will be made are also clearly stated. In World Vision's FMNR Tanzania project (2012–2018), parcels of communal land were handed over to be managed by small FMNR groups which had been formed with project facilitation. In some cases, individuals in the group began acting out of self-interest. They did not contribute their labour and they cut trees without permission. Because by-laws had been established and agreed on from the outset, it was relatively easy to remove offenders from the group. When by-laws are developed in partnership with government stakeholders, group members will have assurance that authorities will support them in upholding the law. Government backing can be a big deterrent to would-be offenders.

Breakthrough in Humbo

A breakthrough in the standing of FMNR within the World Vision partnership came with the implementation of the Humbo, Community Managed Natural Regeneration (CMNR) project, in 2006. This gold standard carbon sequestration project under the Clean Development Mechanism is high profile, involving the World Bank, the Ethiopian government, the Humbo community and World Vision. It was World Vision's first carbon trading project. To many in World Vision, carbon trading represented a potential new income stream for World Vision programming and so Humbo generated much interest. Through this heightened attention, many in the World Vision partnership incidentally became aware of FMNR and its impacts. Thus, Humbo became a catalyst for the spread of FMNR through the World Vision partnership and beyond, as people came from across Ethiopia, neighbouring East African countries and the world to see the transformation. Many came away inspired by what they saw.

The project goal is to regenerate 2,728 hectares of previously degraded forest land, with the aim of enhancing the local communities' livelihoods through improved environmental conditions as well as financial inflows to be achieved thorough linkages with carbon markets.

The total value of the contract is USD 638,000 and carbon revenue to date totals USD 554,680. The project helped communities form cooperatives which have invested these funds wisely. Constructing grain storage facilities has resulted in members being able to obtain a fair price for their grain at harvest time and when market prices are high. When their own food supplies run out, they can purchase grain from the cooperative at less than market price. Purchase and installation of grain mills has reduced the burden on women who previously had to walk long distances to have their grain milled.

Establishing and running a reforestation carbon trading project proved to be complex and expensive and carbon purchasers do not pay the upfront costs of establishing such projects. Developing a proposal, negotiating with government and the carbon purchaser, estimating the carbon base line, delineating different vegetation strata and estimating carbon sequestration rates require technical skill and finance. The current world price for carbon is low, making it unlikely that new forestry carbon projects will be established. The expense and complexity of forest carbon projects excludes farmers not in partnership with sophisticated NGOs from participating in carbon markets.

It is important to manage expectations with any new project, but even more so with high profile projects like this one. Regular follow-up and good communication strategies are necessary. I had repeated many times that if the communities received carbon credits this would be very good and welcome, but the most significant and long-lasting benefits would be direct: changed microclimate, less flooding, access to firewood and fodder ... Yet, people's focus was on getting the financial credits. The problem with those expectations is that there is a time lag between the start of the project and when carbon credits begin flowing. This caused some consternation in the communities who were poor and often hungry. If delay of payments had continued much longer, the project could have failed. Community leaders acted in faith that World Vision would keep its word, but they took a lot of heat when trying to get the communities to be patient.

To meet strict requirements of carbon purchasers to ensure that carbon stocks will increase without causing deforestation elsewhere, it was necessary to restrict human activities in the reforestation area. To minimize negative impact of poor households reliant on the site, a social mitigation plan was developed before project implementation. The most vulnerable community members were identified along with those whose livelihoods would be impacted by forest closure. This group was especially targeted once the project commenced. Grain was provided through a "Food for Work" programme and in the early stages of the project, negatively impacted individuals were given employment as forest guards, in tree nurseries and in road construction. Small loans were made available for micro enterprise start-ups such as beekeeping, tailoring and small trades. Such interventions not only compensated for any perceived losses, but in many cases individuals' economic circumstances greatly improved.

As the trees grew, new problems arose. Seen from the air, in the dry season Humbo stands out as a caterpillar-shaped blob of dark green surrounded by denuded red earth plains. It was inevitable that the restored site would become a magnet for wildlife. Hardest hit are the farmers close to the forest. Monkeys and wild pigs raid their crops and they must keep a vigil to protect them. There are instances of goats being taken by wild cats (perhaps a leopard) and people have been attacked. Fortunately, cooperatives have carbon finances that they use to compensate farmers with, but the issue of human and wildlife conflict is not fully resolved today. The government wants to make sure that wildlife is protected. Some community members are seeking the right to hunt animals—and perhaps controlled culls would be helpful. Others in the community argue that this would be a big mistake and in no time, there would be no wildlife left. They see potential for new revenue streams through ecotourism. To this end, some community members have received ecotourism training.

For 30 years before project inception, the communities surrounding Humbo mountain were reliant on food aid to one degree or another. Amazingly, only six years after project inception, the seven communities managing the Humbo forest sold 106.7 tonnes of grain to the World Food Programme (WFP). And, in 2016, when much of Ethiopia was ravaged by drought and severe food shortages, communities in Humbo were food secure.

Renewal of People's Dignity

While the impact of FMNR on the environment, livelihoods and food security was both expected and self-evident, in West Africa we noticed the emergence of something else that was just as, if not more significant. With FMNR, or, more accurately, with the implementation of FMNR and all that it involves in mobilizing communities, communication, making work plans, overcoming obstacles, working together towards a common goal, realizing benefits and seeing changes in one's difficult circumstances, we began to see the tangible restoration of hope. People's dignity was being restored before our eyes. Think of how soul destroying it is for a parent to not be able to adequately feed, clothe and educate their children. Year after year of being beaten down by poverty takes its toll, and too many farmers have low self-esteem and see no way out of their predicament. Hopelessness sets in. One of the greatest bonuses I receive for my work is to witness a precious transformation take place as hope is restored. People are being liberated. They begin to believe in themselves, gain confidence and plan for the future. They begin to invest in new farming methods and improvements which will enhance benefits even more.

While I was winding up 18 years of work in Niger I received some Canadian visitors who wanted to see the work. I took them to a village and, before going out to the field, we sat in the shade of the village meeting tree. Gradually people came out and sat around us. I asked them what was the most significant thing that the project I managed had accomplished. I thought they would mention famine relief, after all, lives were saved and the assistance enabled them to stay home, farm and harvest a crop the following season. Or perhaps the well we had dug. Women used to spend hours each day drawing water from unlined wells in danger of collapsing at any time. Fuel-efficient stoves? Zai (compost) pits that could double crop yields? Fast-growing, drought-tolerant acacia trees with nutritious edible seeds? To my surprise, they did not mention any of these. Surely, I thought, they would mention FMNR? In just a few short years they had witnessed the restoration of a windswept, barren landscape. The risk of crop failure had been greatly reduced. There were now alternate income streams. Women could access firewood close at hand and more. No, FMNR was not mentioned.

Initially, I was disappointed. But what they went on to say touched me profoundly. They said, Mr Tony, before this project came we were as nothing. We were nobody. All we saw of our own district chief was the dust from his Land Rover as he sped through our village. The only time we saw a government forestry agent was when they came to fine us for cutting down trees. And all we knew of the outside world was what we heard on the BBC. But nobody knew or cared about us. Today, because of this project we are known. We are somebody. Our district chief now calls on us for advice. The forestry agents hold us up as an example for all of Niger to follow. And, the world—people from Canada, the U.S., Australia, Europe come to see us to learn how we did it. They had found their voice in the world. They had earned respect. They had become proud of who they were. This was the most significant thing.

I believe that to a very large degree, no matter how skilfully crafted our project plan is, it is the ability to demonstrate a connection between FMNR and people's aspirations, sense of self-worth and dignity that will determine whether a movement is created or not. What happened in Niger was not a technological breakthrough and it was not reliant on enormous injections of money. It was a people's breakthrough. We will be successful at restoring the vast areas of the world's degraded farm and forest land when we learn to walk alongside those whose livelihoods depend on these areas, and together learn how to repair and maintain them, all the while restoring peoples' sense of pride and self-worth in the process.

FMNR is Now a Widely Scaled-Up Agricultural Practice in the Drylands: A Robust Legacy of Tony Rinaudo's Career

Dennis Garrity

Introduction

Tony Rinaudo had an epiphany in Niger in the mid-1980s about the power of Farmer Managed Natural Regeneration (FMNR) to be a transformative practice for the African drylands. His journey to build on that epiphany, as described in the previous chapters of this book, was a powerful awakening. But it was not the most significant aspect of his journey—and of the impact of his work. What was most significant was his sheer determination and lifelong dedication to sharing the implications of that experience—initially in the pilot villages in Maradi, Niger, and then far and wide in Africa and around the world. This is what has made that 'discovery' so globally important today. Tony has made it his life's work to inspire thousands of farmers, and hundreds of fellow professionals, about the potential of this transformative practice; such that today, FMNR is generally recognized as a foundational practice for a more productive and sustainable dryland agriculture in countries throughout Africa, Asia and the tropics worldwide. It was that perseverance which made all the difference.

FMNR is a practice that directly confronts the conventional paradigm of agriculture: that crops ought to be produced in clean, treeless fields. But such a new paradigm must be based on a very sound validation—by farmers' experience and by science. That validated knowledge base has been accumulating in the decades following the epiphany in Niger. The evidence base is growing rapidly. There is now solid documentation of the millions of families that are successfully practising Farmer Managed Natural Regeneration on their farms, and in their community forest and grazing lands. And there is also a growing body of research literature that has validated farmer observations about the multi-dimensional benefits of this practice. This chapter delves further into both topics: what does science tell us about why the practice has such widespread potential, and what does the record of accelerating FMNR uptake in other countries tell us about its extremely wide-scale potential for future adoption?

The Context

Interest in the development of the African drylands has increased in recent years. This has been driven mainly by the recognition that these areas were the target of considerable humanitarian aid over the last three decades. Currently, they are the cause of great concern about rising insecurity and conflict. But comparatively little effort has been put into their development to increase people's resilience and address insecurity and dependency on aid. The reawakened interest has translated into support for livestock and crop-based development pathways, and efforts to foster resilient livelihoods revolving around agricultural commodities. Such efforts, however, will be of limited impact without attention to a broader systems approach, which builds on the synergies that trees provide in these systems, and is based on a crop-tree-livestock perspective.

Dryland peoples and their communities have acquired, through the millennia, considerable resilience to overcome the challenges that they face. This enables them to recover following droughts, and other nature-induced shocks like floods and fires. However, the recent very high rate of human population growth in the drylands, along with the increasing frequency and intensity of droughts, are seriously undermining the resilience of both the land and the people.

In the agricultural domain, production of the most important dryland crops is already typically associated with dispersed trees in the farm fields. This form of land use is referred to as agroforestry parklands in the Sahelian context (Boffa 1999). Variants of the parkland system are also common in the Eastern and Southern Africa drylands (Dewees 1995).

Often, trees in these systems directly provide an important product such as wood, gum, oil or fruit. In addition, they provide an input into the production of other major products, such as foliage used as fodder for meat and milk production, tree nectar for honey and tree leaves as bio-fertilizers for improved soil health and crop production. A considerable number of well-recognized tree species and products are associated with the African drylands. These include the baobab tree (*Adansonia digitata*), which provides nutritious fruits and leaves; the shea tree (*Vitellaria paradoxa*) that provides oil used in cooking and in chocolate as well as cosmetics; gum arabic (*Acacia senegalensis*) that provides a gum that is used in many beverages and food items; and the acacia tree *Faidherbia albida*, which enriches soils and provides valuable pods and foliage for fodder. The environmental services derived from trees on farmlands provide another significant stream of benefits, such as soil and water conservation, and a more favourable microclimate for crops to withstand wind, heat and drought stress.

Tree-based systems provide regenerative or restorative effects that are realized at a landscape scale. They cover a wide range of practices that enrich the quality of the land resource and they provide additional environmental benefits such as watershed protection and enhanced biodiversity. The natural regeneration of trees may be applied across the entire range of land use types, including farmlands, forests, woodlands and rangelands. Restoration at scale has been achieved through the efforts of millions of rural residents across many countries. Examples include the evergreening of the farmlands in Niger, Mali, Senegal and Malawi as well as the large-scale watershed rehabilitation efforts in Ethiopia.

Opportunities to reduce vulnerability and increase resilience

It is important to distinguish between systems that are based on tree regeneration practices and those that are based on the purposeful planting and/or management of certain trees. The natural regeneration of trees leads to the emergence and use of a diversity of indigenous species that generate a range of products and services. In the drier areas of sub-Saharan Africa, natural regeneration accounts for an overwhelming majority of the trees that are being managed by farmers (greater than 90%).

These regenerative practices include Farmer Managed Natural Regeneration of trees (FMNR) in croplands and Assisted Natural Regeneration (ANR) through enclosures that rehabilitate rangelands or woodlands. They are based on the local selection and management of a diverse range of tree species that are well adapted to the local conditions and they entail very low establishment costs. They are currently being expanded on large areas throughout the arid and semi-arid drylands, and they are now seen as foundational systems for application throughout these agro-ecosystems. It is important to emphasize that the regeneration of trees on farms may occur throughout the farm, including in crop fields as well as on field boundaries. The result is a mosaic of trees that are integrated into land uses such as cropping, pastures and fallows.

The purposeful planting and management of certain types of tree species that can produce economically valuable products and services is also important. Tree planting is particularly widespread in the more sub-humid and humid zones, where rainfall is greater and tree survival is more successful. In these zones the risk of poor seedling survival, or of losing more mature trees due to drought, is less pronounced and the productivity of individual planted trees is also higher—thus, compensating for the greater costs of establishing them by planting from nursery-raised seedlings.

Farmer Managed Natural Regeneration and Assisted Natural Regeneration

Farmer Managed Natural Regeneration (FMNR) on agricultural lands and Assisted Natural Regeneration (ANR) on community lands provide the most cost-effective way of achieving a widespread increase in numbers of valuable, adapted and diverse trees. These practices have in common that people (individual farmers or entire communities) actively influence the natural biological regeneration processes in order to achieve tree patterns that better suit their needs. On agricultural lands, farmers identify naturally regenerating tree seedlings or sprouted rootstocks in their fields. They protect and manage them to provide various benefits (for direct products or to enhance crop or livestock production). On community lands, local groups may adopt the same practices and they may also introduce grazing management systems at the community level that are designed to allow successful tree regeneration in the targeted areas. Under both systems protecting the young trees, weeding around them and pruning them as they grow may be necessary to help them survive and flourish.

In recent years, FMNR has gained in popularity in many dryland areas in western, eastern and southern Africa. Because it requires very little or no cash investment, FMNR can expand rapidly through farmer-to-farmer and village-to-village diffusion. The case of Niger, which Tony Rinaudo initially spearheaded, provides the most dramatic example of how quickly and how extensively the practice can spread (Reij et al. 2009). But Niger is just the tip of the iceberg. A recent study carried out in Niger, Mali, Burkina Faso and Senegal has found that almost all farmers are now actively regenerating trees on their farms (Place and Binam, 2013).

Tree-based systems for natural resource management

The products and services derived from FMNR vary from location to location, depending on the tree species that are present in the area and are valued by farmers. Throughout the Sahel more than 100 different woody species are being managed by farmers through natural regeneration. These trees provide a high level of value to local people (Place and Binam, 2013). They contribute products for human consumption (more than USD 200 per household per year) and fodder for livestock during the late dry season. They also have positive effects on crop yield—accounting for roughly 15–25% increased millet and sorghum yields. Trees provide many environmental services, including carbon sequestration, watershed protection and soil health enrichment. These services can be generated either through FMNR, Assisted Natural Regeneration (ANR) or by purposeful tree planting. All trees sequester carbon at a relatively stable proportion of 0.5 of their woody biomass dry weight. Tree growth is slower in more arid environments. The annual above-ground carbon sequestration from a typical regenerated field may be around 1 tonne per hectare in the semi-arid regions with an additional third of that below ground. These systems supply a large amount of nitrogen very cheaply. They also benefit soils in many other ways such as soil carbon build-up and improved soil physical structure.

A livelihood is classified as sustainable when it can cope with—and recover from—stresses and shocks. In addition, it needs to maintain or enhance family assets and capabilities, both now and in future, while not undermining the natural resource base (DFID 2000). Livelihoods in the drylands are affected by a number of natural hazards. Repetitive drought is the most prominent one. Others include floods as well as animal and human diseases that are often triggered or intensified by droughts and floods. Other factors—such as weak institutions and inappropriate policies—are human-induced hazards. These exacerbate the impacts of the natural hazards. Conflict is another shock that is increasingly common in dryland areas: witness the prolonged quarter-century of conflict in Somalia, the widespread insecurity in the northern regions of Mali and Niger, in north-eastern Nigeria and throughout the Central African Republic. Drylands are also prone to economic risks that are felt primarily in terms of shortages of food and fodder as well as price spikes for food and inputs during periods of stress.

Vulnerability is often the result of extreme poverty especially where poor people have limited options to sustain their livelihoods. It is also due to exposure to hazards that affect the primary livelihoods of the poor. A typical example from the drylands is when a long-term drought pushes up food prices, worsening the condition of pastoralists' or agropastoralists' livestock and even causing the death of the animals. Rural people may find themselves in a position where it is difficult to sell excess stock to buy food and guard against future hunger in this situation. Or they find that livestock prices have collapsed because many people are disposing of their herds simultaneously. Then they find themselves locked into a massively deteriorating livelihood crisis.

Resilience is a desirable condition, often regarded as the converse of vulnerability, where people have the means to protect themselves from such hazards. But complete protection from exposure to drought, flood and other eco-physical factors is not possible.

Trees reduce exposure to shocks

In the drylands of Africa, there is relatively little that individual households can do to reduce their exposure to shocks, short of moving away from the affected area. If a household is located in a place that is affected by a weather or price shock, it will be exposed. However, many households acting together through collective action can achieve landscape-level effects that do in fact reduce exposure. An example of this is the reduced incidence of weather-induced dust storms in south-central Niger that has occurred due to the widespread regeneration of agricultural landscapes with FMNR. The dust storm frequency and intensity has declined markedly after the communities created a contiguous tree cover over an immense area through FMNR. Farmers also testify that in the absence of tree populations on their fields they were often forced to replant their crops multiple times as high winds bury or kill the emerging crop seedlings. But with regenerated tree populations the wind speeds in the fields are dramatically reduced and planting more than once is no longer necessary.

At the macro level, recent modelling studies have demonstrated that tree-covered landscapes, which have higher evapotranspiration rates, have a tendency to increase rainfall in the landscapes downwind from them (Ent et al., 2010), thus reducing their exposure to drought.

Trees reduce sensitivity to shocks | Trees can play an important role in reducing household sensitivity to shocks. Although trees are not impervious to climate change, their deep rooting systems, which access deeper sources of water, make them less vulnerable to seasonal rainfall reductions. This robustness enables trees to play a particularly important role in reducing sensitivity to at least three important types of shocks: weather-related, climate-related and health-related shocks (Place et al., 2016).

Reduced sensitivity to weather-related shocks | The dominant weather-related shocks are droughts which are unusually severe, frequent or prolonged. Trees in crop fields directly and significantly ameliorate the severity of drought effects on annual crop performance by creating a more favourable microclimate. Crops in the vicinity of trees experience a higher level of humidity in the crop canopy, reducing plant desiccation. Trees also slightly shade the crops, reducing solar over-radiation stress. They also dramatically increase the infiltration and storage of rainfall in the soil by reducing surface run-off (Ilstedt et al., 2016). The additional foliage that trees provide increases the soil organic matter which enhances both soil moisture storage capacity and nutrient availability to the crops. Moreover, there are circumstances in which some trees effectively transfer water from lower depths, bringing it up close to the soil surface through their root systems and making such water available to nearby crops ('hydraulic lift'—Bayala et al., 2014). Together, these phenomena reduce the rate of onset of crop water stress, enabling crops to more successfully withstand periods of drought during the growing season.

Reduced sensitivity to climate-related shocks | Global temperatures are increasing as a result of climate change. Average temperatures in the Sahel have increased by about one degree Celsius during the past 40 years (UNEP 2011). Periods of extreme day-time temperatures are also more frequent and severe. Most annual crops experience a reduction in their yield potential as a result of higher temperatures due to two processes: they have higher respiration rates, which burns up more of their energy, making less of it available for grain filling. And they shorten the crop maturity period (fewer days between flowering and maturity) which also reduces the size and weight of the grain.

Trees in crop fields significantly reduce temperatures in the crop canopy and at the soil surface. This reduces the crop exposure to high temperature shock, particularly at midday. The aggregate effect across the growing season is to reduce the shock of a shortened crop maturity period, thus enabling the crop to photosynthesize longer and to increase the length of the grain-filling period and the ultimate yield (Sida et al., 2018). The sum of these effects of reduced shock sensitivity is a more stable crop yield in drought years in fields with tree populations than in fields without them. Surveys in Niger, comparing the crop performance in drought years between villages and households with and without the practice of Farmer Managed Natural Regeneration of trees, have also provided farm-level evidence that higher tree populations reduce the drought effects on crops (Reij et al., 2009).

Reduced sensitivity to human health shocks | Tree-based systems may reduce a family's sensitivity to health shocks during seasonal or prolonged drought-induced hunger periods. Fruit and vegetable foods from trees are obtained from the farm or from the forest during these periods (Place and Binam, 2013). These products also assist in sustaining and improving nutritional levels, particularly of children. For example, the fruits and leaves of baobab are highly nutritious in vitamins A and C, which are lacking in staple foods (Orwa et al., 2009), or are unavailable from other sources during the dry season.

Trees help to cope with shocks

A diverse portfolio of trees on the farm can enhance a household's ability to cope with stresses because the fruits or edible leaves from different species are available at different times during the year. The leaves from several trees are available as sources of vegetable protein throughout the year, for human or livestock nutrition (e.g. baobab, moringa and others).

In the Maradi and Zinder Regions of Niger, where Tony Rinaudo worked and where 1.2 million households now sustain medium-to-high densities of tree populations on their farms, tree branches are cut on a continuous cycle for household fuelwood supplies and for sale. Some of the mature trees are also cut down and sold in local wood markets for poles and construction materials. Export markets are now active in buying and shipping wood south to Nigeria. During prolonged drought periods, these tree assets may be gradually liquidated to supply the household with cash for food purchases. This process was observed to be an important source of coping capacity for households during prolonged drought (Reij et al., 2009).

Trees are important to the livelihoods of dryland households and can contribute in many ways to resilience. Income from wood and non-wood tree products can make a significant contribution to rural households' budgets and their food security. The services that trees provide for crop and livestock systems are in many cases even more important and of higher value than their direct products alone. Building resilience and improving livelihoods requires an integrated approach. Investment in scaling up FMNR should be seen as an essential component of a basic set of technological options for supporting dryland livelihoods.

During drought years farmers survive on trees because they provide different sources of income. Yamba and Sambo (2012) surveyed in two districts (Kantché and Mirriah) in the Zinder Region of Niger, each with high population densities and high on-farm tree densities. Niger's estimated food deficit in 2011/2012 was 600,000 tonnes. Surprisingly, the Kantché district with 350,000 people had produced a grain surplus of almost 14,000 tonnes in 2011, which was a major drought year. The district had produced significant grain surpluses since 2007.

FMNR and soil fertility

Trees of all types have some properties that are beneficial for soil conservation and fertility, chiefly through their root systems, which help to hold soils in place. But also through their litter that falls as mulch as well as the organic matter that the roots and litter provide to nourish micro and macro fauna in the soil. Many farmers have known and appreciated these properties for generations. At the same time, trees can compete with crops in terms of nutrients, water and light. So, farmers weigh the benefits and costs in associating trees with crops and make decisions on the appropriate tree species, the optimum densities of these trees in their crop fields and the type and severity of pruning that they employ to reduce competition. Trees in crop fields may also interfere with animal ploughing operations, by imposing additional time and costs. Thus, cultivation with 'clean' fields is often the message that extension agents have conventionally conveyed to farmers (Smith, 2010).

Quite a number of tree species have been found to offer significant benefits to soils with relatively little competition with crops. The kingpin for the African drylands is *Faidherbia albida* (formerly *Acacia albida*). It fixes atmospheric nitrogen, has a deep rooting system, a relatively sparse, open canopy and it drops its nitrogen-rich leaves onto the soils right as the rainy season begins. There are many other useful species for soils as well. These are often the same species that are beneficial as livestock fodder (such as many of the acacia species).

A meta-analysis of studies on the effects of fertilizer trees on maize yields found that they often have significant positive effects—generally, a doubling of yields or more (Sileshi et al., 2008). However, results vary and species choice and management are critical factors, as are the local environmental conditions. Two recent studies (Glenn, 2012, Place and Binam, 2013) examined the yield and profit effects from FMNR in Malawi and the Sahel respectively. In both cases, *faidherbia* was a common species, and in the case of Malawi, the dominant species. Both studies found positive effects on yields from the trees alone and on profits as well, due to the low labour requirements. The millet/sorghum yield effects of FMNR were between 16–30% in Mali, Burkina Faso and Niger, controlling for other inputs and conditions (Place and Binam, 2013). In Malawi, Glenn (2012) found that *faidherbia* trees increase maize yields by 12–16%. The limited evidence suggests that—while the fertilizer tree systems cannot completely shield crops from some yield losses in droughts—they provide higher yields than when trees are absent (Akinnifesi et al., 2010).

The extent of FMNR adoption

A key objective of Farmer Managed Natural Regeneration is to create a vegetative cover that is commonly referred to as an agroforestry parkland system. Parklands are generally understood to be landscapes in which mature trees are scattered in cultivated (or recently fallowed) fields (Pullan, 1974; Sautter, 1968, cited in Raison, 1988). The parkland system is the dominant land use system across the entire West African semi-arid and sub-humid zones. In these agroforestry parklands, the composition and density of the woody vegetation is altered by humans in order to optimize its use. Most often, parklands development reflects a continual process of tree species selection, tree density management and tree pruning to optimize the benefits.

Parklands are not limited to the Sahel and Sudanian zones of Africa. Further evidence has been assembled on the widespread use of FMNR by farmers in parts of Ethiopia (Hadgu et al., 2011), Malawi (Dewees, 1995; Kundhlande et al., 2017), Tanzania (Monela et al., 2005), Kenya (Muriuki, 2013; Oginosako et al., 2006) and Zimbabwe (Campbell et al., 1991). There is considerable evidence that farming households in Malawi have encouraged the regeneration of trees in fields and around their households (Dewees, 1995). Recent surveys show that more than 85% of Malawian farmers protect a wide variety of trees regenerating on their land (Nyoka, 2013; Kundhlande et al., 2017).

The term 'agroforestry parkland' emphasizes the multiple forms and purposes of these systems. They differ considerably in terms of three variables: the density of trees and shrubs, the diversity of tree species and the age of individual trees. Together, these shape the economic benefits that can be generated today and in the future. A healthy parkland agroforestry system would include both mature trees that provide benefits today, along with some younger trees to replenish the system for the future. However, demographic, economic, environmental and social developments during the past 40 years have put serious pressure on the traditional land-use systems of the Sahel. Modern Sahelian forest laws that banned the cutting of trees on farms without a licence, and the ways that they are locally enforced, discouraged farmers from engaging in optimum parkland management practices. This led to the degradation of the parklands to a varying extent across the region (Boffa, 1999). It was particularly serious in Niger.

During the 1970s and 1980s, Nigerien farmers faced massive tree losses from drought (affecting particularly the young trees) and human population pressures, resulting in widespread desertification of the agricultural landscape. After conventional reforestation projects failed, as Tony Rinaudo has noted in earlier chapters, the pilot projects that he initiated during the mid-to-late 1980s were followed by larger development projects that began to emphasize FMNR as a way to re-establish useful trees in the desertified agroecosystems of southern Niger (Tougiani et al., 2009). They generated a range of benefits, including a supply of dry-season fodder for livestock, firewood supplies, fruit and medicinal products that farm households could consume or sell. Moreover, several species were retained to enhance soil fertility (Barnes and Fagg, 2003).

Interest in FMNR was further stimulated in the 1990s when the successful experiences of several pilot projects were shared with government policymakers. This encouraged the government to relax the restrictive forestry regulations (Code Forestier) that had severely limited farmer management of their own trees. FMNR landscapes began to spread rapidly. In 2004, the Government of Niger formally recognized the trend by revising the national forestry laws to eliminate the onerous restrictions on the freedom of farmers to manage the trees that they cultivated on their own land.

Tree densities and tree cover in Niger have dramatically increased in recent decades. Analysis of high-resolution images acquired during 2003 to 2008 shows that in the Maradi and Zinder Regions of Niger alone, about 4.8 million hectares of farmlands were regenerated by 2008 through FMNR (Reij et al., 2009). An estimated 1.2 million households were engaged in managing these FMNR systems through their own independent efforts. Many villages now have 10–20 times more trees than 20 years ago and the agricultural landscapes of southern Niger have more than 200 million more trees than they did 30 years ago. Reij et al. (2009) estimate that this transformation has resulted in an average of at least 500,000 tonnes of additional food produced per year, which covers the requirements of 2.5 million people. A more recent mapping of tree cover on farmlands has revealed that FMNR is now being practised on over 7 million hectares in Niger (G. Tappan, 2016, pers. comm.).

The further scaling up of Farmer Managed Natural Regeneration has been spreading to other countries in the Sahel, inspired by the Niger experience. The US Geological Survey recently mapped 450,000 hectares of young, contiguous FMNR on the Seno Plains of eastern Mali (Reij, 2012). This had evolved through a similar process as in Niger and was accelerated during the past 15 years as the enforcement of forestry laws discouraging FMNR were relaxed. FMNR is now also prominent in northern Burkina Faso. Interestingly, some farmers there are managing FMNR in more standard row patterns in order to avoid interference with ploughing operations (R. Bunch, 2012, pers. comm.).

In Senegal, the Serer people have sustained a medium to dense cover of mature *Faidherbia albida* parklands on about 150,000 hectares of farmlands for at least the past few generations. But degradation of the tree and land resources prevailed in much of the rest of the country. The Government recently has revised its agricultural strategy to promote FMNR for land regeneration. This has led to over a dozen FMNR pilot projects that are providing the technical and institutional experience to enable the widespread acceleration of re-greening (Sanogo, 2010; Rinaudo, 2012; Herrmann et al., 2013). World Vision's FMNR project in the Kaffrine region has enabled the adoption of 70,000 hectares of new FMNR.

What has happened since 1994 on Mali's Seno Plains illustrates the importance of forestry legislation. In 1991, Mali's president was toppled by a popular uprising. During that period, many forest agents were thrown out of the villages and some were even killed. They had managed to make themselves very unpopular, for instance, by starting bushfires themselves, while later accusing the villagers of having done so. Since the practice of burning was against the law, the forest agents were subsequently able to impose unjustified fines on the people. In 1994, a new forest law was adopted, which regulated the rights of farmers to on-farm trees, on the condition that the land was not left fallow for more than 10 years. This policy encourages farmers to reduce the number of years that they leave their land fallow and to protect on-farm trees. Due to the high and rapidly growing population on the Seno Plains, most farmers have to cultivate their land permanently, in any event.

A radio station in the small town of Bankass on the Seno Plains, which was funded by the NGO SahelEco, decided to broadcast the contents and implications of the new forest law. The reaction of villagers was: "Does this mean we can refuse access to those who cut our trees with a permit of the forestry service?" The answer was 'yes', and it was also broadcast by the radio station. From that day, farmers refused access to woodcutters and began protecting their on-farm trees (Reij and Garrity, 2016).

It took until 2011 before the scale of the new agroforestry systems on the Seno Plains was fully uncovered. Local staff estimated that they spread over 16,000 hectares. However, Gray Tappan of the US Geological Survey's EROS Data Center in South Dakota used satellite images and mapped the area under medium and high-density agroforestry to be almost 500,000 ha. Until 2011, no one had the slightest idea of the scale of this re-greening process. Field visits have shown that 90% of the trees are less than 20 years old.

Recently, there has been a resurgence of interest by the Heads of State of the Sahelian countries to create a Great Green Wall across the continent. At the 1st African Drylands Conference (Dakar, June 2011), scientists presented evidence underpinning the value of an approach based on a participatory engagement of the local rural populations to expand the farmer-to-farmer dissemination of FMNR region-wide. This was supported by the World Bank and the Global Environment Facility, which are now collaborating with each of the Sahelian countries to invest a pool of USD 1.8 billion to implement land regeneration projects based on these community-based natural resource management systems and other restoration methods. The declaration of the 2nd African Drylands Week, convened by the African Union in August 2014, urged that the drylands development community commit seriously to achieving the goal of enabling every farm family and every village across the drylands of Africa to be practising Farmer Managed Natural Regeneration and Assisted Natural Regeneration by the year 2025.

Due to the continued expansion of agricultural land in the drylands, FMNR is all but assured to play an ever more important role in overall tree management. It can be considered a 'foundational practice' that is relevant for virtually all farming systems in the semi-arid and dry sub-humid dryland zones. It has such a wide recommendation domain because establishment costs are very low. Regeneration has a high success rate due to growth from rootstock and self-seedling establishment, and it involves indigenous species that are well adapted to each site environmentally and climatically. This practice can be integrated with the full range of traditional and improved crop and soil management systems. Other tree-based systems that involve the planting of trees can then be built around the basic FMNR practice, further enriching the species portfolio on the farm. Tony Rinaudo refers to this process as FMNR+.

By contrast, tree planting has more limited niches in the drylands. It is more suited to the sub-humid and humid zones, where rainfall is higher, and where there is access to dry season water to be used in tree nurseries (e.g. proximity to low-lying wetland areas). Tree planting is further encouraged where there are attractive commercial opportunities for specific tree species suitable to the drylands (e.g. *Melia volkensii* in the drylands of Kenya).

Environmental services from FMNR practices

In addition to private benefits from the restoration and regeneration practices, environmental services are also provided to other stakeholders. These may attract payments for such services. Carbon sequestration occurs with tree growth, mainly in the wood of the tree but also in the root system. In the drylands, tree growth is slower than in humid areas. For regeneration practices, where tree densities are low and management is less intensive, one might expect around 1 tonne of carbon accumulation in above-ground biomass per ha per year (Beedy et al., 2014). Trees can also add to soil carbon through their roots and leaves. However, while there is a straightforward relationship between above-ground woody biomass and carbon, it is much more difficult to assess soil carbon build-up. Moreover, soil carbon stability is susceptible to change due to tillage and cropping practices. Thus, in terms of the ability of dryland farmers to benefit from carbon finance schemes, the aboveground carbon sequestration through woody biomass is likely to be the primary focus.

Given a typical carbon value added of 1 tonne/ha, this will generate up to USD 10-15 per tonne of carbon dioxide offset value given current prices. However, due to high transactions costs, only a portion of this amount would make its way to the farmer or community. There are several examples of programmes to compensate local people for protection of existing woodlands that are operating in the drylands (e.g. the UN REDD+ programme), but projects that seek carbon sequestration as a major goal generally favour more humid areas, where biomass growth is faster on a per hectare basis.

Restoration and enclosures also provide water and watershed services. Many of these effects are localized, such as spring and river rejuvenation, and enhanced groundwater supply in valleys. But others are felt further downstream, such as erosion and sedimentation control and aquifer replenishment. A study of woodlands in semi-arid and arid areas found that a canopy cover of 3.5-6% would suffice for conferring the surface run-off regulation benefits of the woodlands on the rest of the land (Shivdenko at al., 2005).

Tree vegetation cover in the drylands may also reduce wind speeds and dust loads. African drylands contribute over 50% of total global atmospheric dust circulation. They have dust concentrations considerably higher than any other region of the world (Engelstaedter et al., 2006). In addition, high child mortality is associated with respiratory illnesses, especially in Africa. This has been partly attributed to exposure to dust (Romieu et al., 2002; Smith et al., 1999).

Finally, the biodiversity benefits have been clearly identified and quantified in many tree restoration interventions. This is well noted in the case of tree species, but also for other flora and fauna. In the case of wildlife-based regeneration or conservation systems, the value of this increased biodiversity can be indirectly quantified in terms of increased tourist receipts. However, for many types of smaller, localized restoration efforts, the biodiversity values (e.g. in pollination or pest regulation services) are known but not well quantified.

Costs of FMNR establishment and scaling up

By definition, FMNR neither requires the effort to acquire germplasm, nor to propagate seeds or cuttings, nor to nurture them into seedlings in tree nurseries. The cash cost of regenerating a tree seedling or root sprout that is already established in the field is essentially zero. New trees emerge from the soil without the need for nurturing or protection. However, protection and maintenance may be required for them to thrive.

The more common establishment costs include the protection of the desired trees—either in the form of micro-protection of individual trees or the protection of larger areas—mainly using wood-based barriers or fences—and the removal of trees that are not desired. Maintenance costs may include weeding and pruning. Weeding is primarily for trees emerging from seed, but it is not needed for those emerging from coppices and roots because these grow rapidly. Pruning and other forms of management of the canopy size and shape is often necessary. This is one of the more demanding labour needs for FMNR, especially as the trees mature—but it is also the source of supply for family fuel-wood. In terms of calculating the actual costs incurred by farmers, one has to consider how common these activities are, how much time or material is spent and what the unit costs are in terms of time or materials.

Although the scaling up of FMNR in the Sahel has been labelled as farmer-driven, with little external support, a number of programmes are now investing in the scaling up of FMNR. These programmes are spending resources on enhancing farmer awareness of the benefits of FMNR, building farmer tree management skills, organizing landscape management of grazing and fire, developing tree product markets and identifying workable solutions to forest code regulations. The increased rural population, coupled with dwindling woodland, also suggests that woodland management is not an alternative to FMNR but rather a highly complementary activity (Shumba et al., 2010; Mayaux et al., 2004).

Projects in Niger since 1985 have invested significant resources in the promotion of re-greening by farmers. Part of the 7 million ha of adoption is the direct result of this intervention, but a much larger part is the result of farmers spontaneously adopting the practice because they have observed the benefits and do not need any external support in getting started on their own. What kinds of activities have been funded by donor and government-supported projects? One key activity was the organization of farmer-to-farmer study visits. Letting farmers (men and women) who don't yet use the practice visit those who have gained experience with it, is one of the most effective ways of spreading the practice widely.

The International Fund for Agricultural Development (IFAD) recently calculated the costs of farmer managed re-greening in the Maradi Region. The costs amounted to 9,000 CFA/ha, which is USD 14 per hectare at current exchange levels (USD 1 = CFA 607) (Guéro Chaïbou, pers. comm.).

The impacts of FMNR on household income and food security

The three main sources of private household benefits for practising FMNR are through direct human consumption of tree products, indirect benefits on crop production and increased benefits through livestock production.

In terms of direct consumption benefits from trees, the major products are foods (fruits, nuts, oils and leaves) and wood (construction and fuel-wood). A recent four-country study in the Sahel across 1,000 farms found that all households harvested tree products for their consumption, and in many locations, the quantity and value was high (Place and Binam, 2013). The average harvested value per household ranged from a low of about USD 110 in Senegal to about USD 250 in Niger. Only a minority of harvested products were sold by households for income—the highest being about 35% in Burkina Faso, and the lowest being about 4% in Niger. Burkina Faso households benefit from the presence of a wide distribution of *Vitellaria paradoxa* (shea butter) which has a large and expanding global market.

Crop yield improvement is another major benefit pathway of trees. It is important to note that in the Sahelian countries chemical fertilizer use is low, both in terms of percentage of farmers (25–30%) and amounts applied. Manure is a much more common input (55–80% of farmers). Trees are found throughout all farms, but the density and age profile of those with known beneficial effects on soils ('fertilizer trees') varies across sites. Both are important, for it is the older trees which have the most significant effect on yields. In Niger, the average number of mature fertilizer trees per hectare was 32, while in Mali and Burkina Faso it was lower, at about five per hectare. After controlling for other effects (rainfall, soil type, seed density, area, manure, fertilizer), it was found that the mature fertilizer trees alone increased cereal crop yields by 15-30% in Niger, Mali and Burkina Faso. Furthermore, there is a positive correlation between the presence of mature fertilizer trees and the amounts of manure and fertilizer applied. Thus, farmers tend to apply more manure and fertilizer on fields with a higher density of trees, probably because crop response to these inputs is higher in fields that have a restored soil environment with trees.

Haglund et al. (2011) undertook a study of more than 400 farmers in Niger, comparing those who practise FMNR with those who don't. Their figures indicated that the gross value of crop production for farms practising natural regeneration was USD 138 compared to USD 88 for those that do not practise natural regeneration.

Reij, Tappan and Smale (2009) conservatively estimated that average grain yields had increased by 100 kg/ha on the 5 million ha of new agroforestry parkland. They postulated that the yield increases were higher in the portion of the area that was dominated by *Faidherbia albida*. In this way, re-greening by farmers was calculated to contribute an estimated annual increase in grain production of 500,000 tonnes per year. This is enough grain to feed 2,500,000 people.

FMNR also contributes in other ways to household food security. Some tree species produce fodder, which allows smallholder farmers to keep more livestock. In Niger, livestock now depends on tree fodder for half of the year. Having more livestock means that farmers have more 'cash on the hoof' which they can sell in drought years. In those drought years, farmers sometimes literally survive on trees. They can cut some of their trees and sell them on the market for firewood or construction wood to generate cash which allows them to buy cereals (Reij and Garrity, 2016).

The sale of leaves and fruit generates important income for women. One mature baobab (*Adansonia digitata*) can generate an additional annual income of USD 34–75. This level of revenue allows a family to purchase 70–175 kg of grain on the market. As many as 75 baobab trees may be found growing on 1 ha in some places (Yamba and Sambo, 2012).

The income from the sale of firewood has an estimated average annual value in the Sahel of USD 127–154 per household. The sale of non-timber products, such as fruit alone, can return an average of USD 237 per year, or an additional value of USD 0.66 per day per household (Place and Binam, 2012, quoted by Francis and Weston, 2015).

Individual farmers can protect and manage trees, but it is more effective if village communities organize themselves to do so, and develop enforceable by-laws for protecting and managing the trees. This was done by an project in the Maradi region which was funded by the International Fund for Agricultural Development (IFAD) and supported the building of village institutions. Men and women farmers, but also representatives of the herders, are members of the management committee. The committee holds meetings with surrounding villages (an inter-village organization) to foster cooperation in tree protection. They have developed rules and set fines for the illegal cutting of trees. And these rules are enforced.

Can an increase in rainfall in the Sahel explain the emergence of agroforestry parklands?

It has been argued that it was the general increase in rainfall in the Sahel that was the major cause for the large-scale re-greening in Southern Niger. Average rainfall in the Sahel has indeed increased since the mid-1980s, after a prolonged cycle of drought years. It is true that this increase in rainfall has had a positive impact on natural regeneration and on the growth of woody species. But if rainfall were the determining factor for re-greening, then on-farm tree densities in Northern Nigeria should be higher than in Southern Niger, since they have similar population densities, similar soils and the same ethnic population. Northern Nigeria has more rainfall, but has much lower on-farm tree densities than Southern Niger. The conclusion that can be drawn is that rainfall facilitates the regeneration of woody species, but it is the deliberate human choices and management of naturally regenerated trees that is a more important determining factor than rainfall.

According to van Noordwijk et al. (2015) new evidence is emerging about the positive effects of forests and trees on rainfall. If this is the case, the large-scale development of new agroforestry parklands in Southern Niger may have had some positive impact on rainfall, particularly in areas downwind of the extensive parklands in Zinder and Maradi regions. However, the rainfall data for this region have not yet been fully analyzed to examine this possibility.

Why does large-scale natural regeneration by farmers fly under the radar?

The examples from Niger and Mali show that the significance of even large-scale FMNR can go unrecognized at the national and regional levels. This has also proven to be the case in Malawi. The scale at which farmers had protected and managed natural regeneration was revealed only recently. Why is it that outsiders have not observed it? Is it because farmers on their own played such a dominant role, and that no project signboard was put up next to it? Could it also be a case of 'hidden in plain view'? Authorities are not expecting or looking for a solution to come from uneducated farmers, and they do not immediately recognize this as a valid, albeit unconventional way of solving a pressing problem that has vexed and eluded the experts.

Is it not likely that more FMNR successes remain to be uncovered?

Scaling up FMNR

There are several institutional-related factors that limit the potential for FMNR, such as fire setting, free grazing and the rights and regulations over trees. The use of fire and free grazing systems generate benefits to some local people—in terms of grass regeneration, clearing of debris, catching wild rodents for food, and in the case of free grazing, offering a cheap mechanism for feeding livestock. Place and Binam (2013) found that a large percentage of Sahelian farmers feel that unreasonable forest codes are still a limiting factor (44%). They also identify other important constraints as the heavy-handedness on the part of forest officers (38%), uncontrolled cutting of trees by outsiders (31%) and animal damage (28%) from uncontrolled grazing.

It is challenging to deploy institutional reforms that can reconcile the interests of FMNR practitioners with the interests of others who benefit from setting fires and practising free grazing. This points to the need for consultations and engagement with all stakeholders in the community. Fortunately, practices such as controlled fires, rotational grazing areas and the promotion of livestock corridors are all options that have been successfully implemented in the drylands to facilitate the scaling up of FMNR. So we know that these challenges can be overcome.

The issue of forest regulations that create disincentives for farmers is one constraint that is widespread in the developing world. These include bans on the felling or cutting of a number of species without obtaining a prior permit, at a fee. Violation of such regulations entails a hefty fine. Farmers will often remove young trees from their land to avoid having to adhere to these rules in the future. Among such regulations, the adverse effects of the Sahelian forest codes have long been recognized (e.g. McLain, 1992). There have been many policy dialogues in the region to try and move reforms forward. Although not initially backed by formal policy change, the recent re-greening in Niger and Mali has been attributed to a significant extent by the relaxation of the enforcement of such policies (Reij et al., 2009). A recent analysis of the forest codes and recommendations for action was done by Yatich et al. (2013).

The existence (or not) of markets for tree products is another factor that impacts on incentives to establish and manage trees. The development of tree product markets has a positive effect on encouraging tree-based systems in general. For FMNR in particular, market development may have different effects. In general, as these markets develop, there is more incentive to maintain trees on farms, as the case of shea in Burkina Faso has demonstrated. There may be further incentives that influence the selection of tree species to retain in the crop fields, based on market signals, but only if market signals persist for a long enough period, since changes in tree species composition is a long-term evolutionary proposition in the drylands.

FMNR should be recommended in all geographical regions in Africa, particularly in the semi-arid and dry sub-humid drylands. There is a vast area of cropland between 400–1,000 mm of annual rainfall which includes large areas of the West African Sahel, the Horn of East Africa and much of Southern Africa (table 1). The key foundational agroforestry

Table 1 | Dryland zones in sub-Saharan Africa where FMNR is particularly suitable. [Source: R. Winterbottom et al. 2013.]

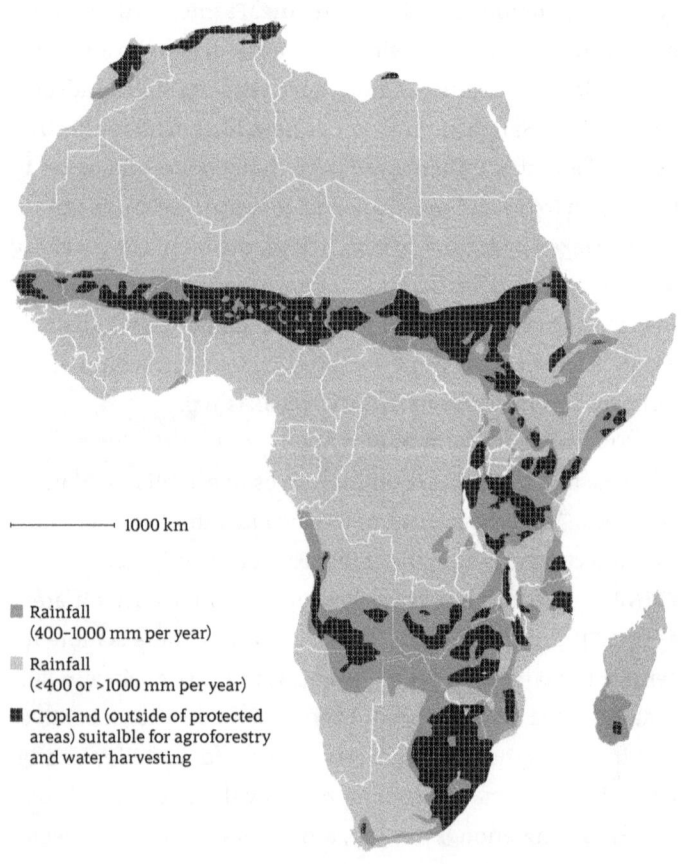

practice for these zones is Farmer Managed Natural Regeneration, for use on all farms in the zone, complemented by other improved farming practices as well as cropping and livestock systems. Place and Binam (2013) found that over 90% of trees on farms in the Sahelian countries were established by Farmer Managed Natural Regeneration.

There is growing political support for massively scaling up FMNR. The World Resources Institute, the German Development Cooperation (GIZ), the African Union and a number of other organizations are now jointly supporting a process of engaging many countries in Africa to restore 100 million hectares of degraded landscapes by 2030. This AFR100 initiative has an audacious level of ambition that can only be achieved if FMNR, led by farmers and their communities, will be a dominant component of the effort. No other set of practices could possibly accomplish the job—given the enormous areas of land involved and the limited investment funds available.

The World Resources Institute recently published a report about how to scale up re-greening successes (Reij and Winterbottom, 2015). This report builds on and distils the re-greening experiences observed in the West African Sahel that were discussed above. The scaling strategy has six steps, and some activities under each of the steps.

Step 1: Identify and analyze re-greening successes
There are many small and large re-greening successes in Africa's drylands. As the examples from Niger and Mali show, re-greening by farmers is often overlooked. Each country should make an effort to identify its previous re-greening successes, because these can be sources of inspiration and training grounds for farmers who do not yet protect and manage their naturally regenerating trees.

Step 2: Build a grassroots movement
In most countries, donor-funded projects are already promoting some forms of participatory natural resource management, but they are not always working together. The challenge is to unite them in order to create synergies and stronger poli-

tical leverage in collaboration with government and to expand enabling policies and legislation.

Farmer-to-farmer study visits are a very effective way of scaling up FMNR. In some regions, both women and men farmers have gained so much experience with the practices that they have become experts and can train others. These hubs provide the foundation for outward expansion. If it is true that practice precedes policy, then it is important to inform government about the successes and about the existing dynamics that can accelerate the process on-the-ground.

Step 3: Address policy and legal issues and improve the enabling conditions

Working at the grassroots level only is not sufficient to accelerate the scaling up of FMNR. The role of national governments is to create forestry legislation and agricultural development policies that induce land users to invest in trees. Current forest legislation tends to show some weaknesses. One of these is that they often do not recognize farmers' rights to own, manage and harvest the trees that are established on their land. For instance, in most Sahelian countries, farmers are allowed to exploit and also cut the trees that they have planted, but if they have protected and managed natural regeneration of indigenous tree species, they may need a permit from the forestry service in order to manage, prune or harvest the trees.

A major weakness that needs to be addressed is that Ministries of Environment tend to be interested in natural forests and in planting trees, but not in natural regeneration; whereas Ministries of Agriculture usually concentrate their extension efforts only on annual crops. However, as soon as funding for agroforestry projects becomes available, turf fights often emerge between both ministries. The Ministries of Environment then claim that agroforestry is about trees, which is their domain, while the Ministries of Agriculture, which have much stronger extension services—and usually have a much greater capacity to implement such projects—claim that it is all about farming systems. The solution is the development of inter-sectoral platforms that combine the strengths of both ministries in the accelerated scaling up of agroforestry.

Step 4: Develop and implement an effective communications strategy

It is possible to reach out to tens of millions of smallholders by using rural and regional radio stations to spread the messages about re-greening and by linking mobile phones with radio as well as ICT to make the web more accessible to rural people. The process can be enhanced by inviting national and international journalists to visit re-greening successes. However, at this moment most re-greening projects don't have a communications strategy, or if they have one, it is seriously underfunded. The challenge is to inform all land users in a country about what has been achieved and what they and their communities can do to participate. Land users themselves should be at the heart of FMNR communications strategies.

Step 5: Develop or strengthen FMNR tree product value chains

This is where the private sector has a major role to play. They can support the development of value chains around the agroforestry products from FMNR. This will put more cash into the pockets of smallholder farmers and induce them to expand their tree enterprises.

Step 6: Design research activities to fill gaps in knowledge about FMNR

We know enough to move into accelerated action on FMNR scaling up, but at the same time it is important to fill some important gaps in our knowledge. For instance, too little is known about the impact of landscape-level FMNR on surface and groundwater hydrology, or about the impact of re-greening on rainfall, on carbon sequestration in biomass or in soils and on nutrition as well as food security.

Conclusion

FMNR has great potential to reduce vulnerability and increase the resilience of households living in the dryland regions of sub-Saharan Africa. This potential is not always appreciated. Work remains to be done to change the mindsets of policymakers, development professionals and even technical specialists such as researchers and extension agents. For many, mixing trees with crops is considered unconventional, even backward and to be avoided. Yet a growing body of evidence suggests that successfully integrating trees into farming and livestock keeping activities can be extremely profitable, provided the appropriate species and management practices are used.

Tony Rinaudo's epiphany about FMNR in Niger back in the mid-1980s and his steady persistence in building awareness and expanding training efforts across many countries have inspired the scaling-up efforts that we see taking root in Africa and across the world. They set the stage for the development of an EverGreen Agriculture Partnership in 2012 that has grown into a strong alliance of development NGOs and international organizations, governments, research and educational institutions and the private sector. The Partnership (evergreen-agriculture.net) is championing all aspects of the scaling up of FMNR, as part of a vision to fully exploit the potential for trees to be integrated into agriculture and forest and rangeland systems around the world. It is now evolving into an evergreening alliance that is mobilizing a powerful global movement on land restoration and supports national evergreening movements everywhere. That's a pretty significant legacy for a humble guy that stumbled unexpectedly onto a very big idea.

"Trust Would Be a Good Starting Point"

Interview with Günter Nooke

Günter Nooke (age 59) is the Commissioner for Africa in the German Federal Ministry for Economic Cooperation and Development (BMZ) as well as German Chancellor Angela Merkel's Personal Representative for Africa. He met Tony Rinaudo during a seven-day trip that World Vision Deutschland had organized for friends and supporters of the Farmer Managed Natural Regeneration (FMNR) method. The group was travelling at the height of the dry season in late March 2017 both in Humbo in south-western Ethiopia as well as in Tigray in the Abyssinian Highlands in north-eastern Ethiopia. In conversation with Johannes Dieterich, Nooke discusses FMNR, reforestation, energy supply, population growth and his perception of development policy.

JOHANNES DIETERICH | *You and Tony Rinaudo have reviewed his FMNR projects together in Ethiopia. What was your impression?*

GÜNTER NOOKE | At first, I'm sure my reaction was like many others: Tony Rinaudo's personality made the biggest impression on me. Some people transmit so much positive energy that even such naturally rational characters like me cannot avoid being influenced by this—and we wouldn't want to. It's simply a pleasure to follow Tony's knowledgeable and dedicated instructions as he carefully prunes the young bushes with his knife in his hand to let small tree stumps rapidly sprout and re-grow independently, so helping to restore the most karstified valley.

Has this positive impression already influenced the policy adopted by Germany's Federal Government? Does the Government support the FMNR projects—and if so, in what way?

The Government has discussed FMNR; the Parliamentary State Secretary has taken a personal and lively interest in it. Unfortunately, this has not influenced our bilateral portfolio with Ethiopia so far. But I'm very pleased that the European Union is introducing programmes that will support and encourage FMNR. State development cooperation as well as NGOs' development projects often suffer from the fact that they are not only 'developed' from a Western perspective, but also meant to create well-paid jobs for many Western development aid workers or 'expats'. We must think differently about this—and I'm sure this is coming. The question is only: how quickly.

As part of the African Forest Landscape Restoration Initiative (AFR100) led by the African Union more than 100 million hectares of land in Africa are earmarked for restoration. Is the Federal Government involved in this initiative?

The restoration of forests is one of the three pillars of our forest action plan. The AFR100-initiative was launched in December 2015 in Paris by the Federal Ministry for Economic Cooperation and Development (BMZ) together with other international organizations. By 2030, 100 million hectares across Africa should be restored creating forests and wooded, productive landscapes. So far 26 countries have joined in the initiative and identified an area of approximately 86 million hectares. Our concern at the BMZ is also to make a visible international contribution to the implementation of such goals—like the restoration of the forests. AFR100 is effective at the interfaces of climate, alleviating poverty and improving environmental performance (water, soil and bio-diversity) and it makes a direct contribution to realizing the goals for sustainable development and the three Rio Conventions. Germany's governmental funding for AFR100 stands currently at about EUR 32 million. Moreover, the Government is committed to implementing measures in Ethiopia, Cameroon, Madagascar and Togo.

Has the 'discovery' of FMNR methods already influenced the Federal Government's strategy for development policy? For example, is less expenditure earmarked for projects to plant new trees?

Starting with the pioneering successes of the FMNR approach in Niger, the method is increasingly being used in several countries in the Sahel region, but also in Ethiopia and Southern Africa. In principle, I am no critic of development cooperation initiatives. In fact, I'm certain that we're moving in the right direction and not repeating past mistakes. However, in view of the immense challenges things take far too long—stopping the acknowledged mistakes, reinforcing methods that work and developing new measures that, in my opinion, also include FMNR.

What relative value do you assign to the FMNR method in counteracting the effects of climate change? Can it effectively deal with its symptoms—higher temperatures and more severe droughts?

Reforestation and restoring the woodland is not only important for the global climate system. Trees in the agricultural landscape, particularly in arid environments, are increasingly important for the micro- and local climate. We must present our arguments more carefully and not justify every weather phenomenon due to climate change. It's especially helpful for farmers, if their plant cultures are exposed to less heat stress entirely regardless of how this is achieved.

Could reforestation also contribute to the reduction of the proportion of CO_2 in the atmosphere—so, not only counteracting the symptoms of global warming?

Of course, FMNR like every measure to restore landscapes makes an important contribution to this. In Africa during the past century the degradation of the rainforest has become more severe; this is primarily associated with population growth and cutting down trees for firewood. Under such conditions there is no question of relying on sustainable forestry like in Europe.

Tony Rinaudo's experiences show that it's not easy for the rural population in Africa to earn carbon credits for their reforestation initiatives on the carbon trading market. Should politicians not help more in this area?

I'm not sure whether it would be appropriate to make a monetary settlement for local climate protection measures and then to argue about the level of allocated contributions for restoration projects as well as the associated payments. I would prefer responsible governments that get engaged in international measures. The old idea that the atmosphere's capacity for carbon disposal is limited and must be divided fairly among all populations leads to mandatory financial compensation from the North to the South because, for example, in Germany we use twice as much as our allocation. At the same time, however, a country like Nigeria would have an incentive to reduce its harmful climate emissions by burning off associated gases made in oil production. These are still higher than all the other CO_2 emissions in Nigeria produced by households, traffic, agriculture and—if it exists at all—industry.

In large parts of Africa, the energy supply is still so precarious that especially in rural regions the people have no alternative other than burning wood. Do you see any opportunities to change this?

Worldwide, currently about 2.7 billion people are still primarily dependent on wood as an energy source and most of them live in developing countries. In Sub-Saharan Africa, 80% of the population is reliant on wood as an energy source. Not least because of population growth the demand for wood to provide energy will continue to rise in developing countries. This creates substantial problems if it is not achieved sustainably and the forests continue to be severely degraded. Strategies for solutions are based on sustainable wood production and efficient consumption.

In Germany, for three centuries people have been aware of the importance of the sustainable use of wood for fuel. At the start of the 18th century, Hans Carl von Carlowitz, the chief mining official in Saxony, warned of the disastrous consequences of burning wood. Why has this knowledge not become more widespread?

That's true: Baron von Carlowitz already defined the principle of sustainability in 1713. Accordingly, only as many tree logs should be taken from a forest as can regrow. This simple yet pioneering idea dates from the era of the large-scale destruction of the forest in Germany due to unregulated and over-intensive use for fuel, building and especially mining timber. The conservation of timber was an economic interest. Perhaps, nowadays on some subjects—or how we discuss them—too much emphasis is placed on ideology. And this is rarely convincing.

Solar energy seems made for Africa with its extended hours of sunshine. But here the technology is only being adopted very slowly. Why?

Well, now we should have a long talk about the special conditions in Africa while being cautious about generalizations because things work very differently in the individual countries. In rural regions for many years development organizations have offered solar-powered stoves for cooking which in fact prove unpopular. Often, we spend too little time getting to know the cultural context and traditional behavioural patterns; we're surprised when our interventions aren't accepted. Meanwhile, traditions and customs, which evolved and were handed down over centuries, coincide with state-of-the-art modern digital solutions. Although a great deal is possible, we must bring people on board with respect for their culture and religion. For me, this means not conveying the idea that things mustn't change. At the same time, however, we must also realize that there can be no permanent achievements without insights into the respective community's attitudes and therefore the inability to change them. This is also known as the fourth, cultural dimension of sustainability.

In Sub-Saharan Africa, solar energy is especially important for power generation. This includes the use of decentralized, networked solar systems to locations outside the power supply network. Photovoltaic technology may still prove too expensive for African standards. However, this is gradually changing.

The rumour is that agriculture in Africa has the potential to make a significant contribution to the development of the continent—some experts claim it's even more important than industrialization. If this is the case, the restoration of soil fertility plays an even more significant role. In this context, should FMNR not be encouraged even more passionately?

As mentioned, I'm a strong supporter of FMNR. However, my advisors have convinced me that nothing will advance in

Africa without industrialization. Agriculture tends to follow rather than being a step ahead of industrialization—for instance, thanks to the effective use of soil fertility and cultivation methods as well as processing farm products.

With its vast areas that are suitable for agricultural use Africa is also of interest to international companies with the aim of procuring extensive cultivation areas on the continent. Is this a welcome development? Or does it involve a risk both for African agriculture as well as for soil regeneration?

There are opportunities and risks in this context as well as positive and negative examples. In Africa, agricultural production is well below its potential. There is a massive requirement for investment. A commercial, technological and modern agrarian economy can contribute considerably to the local and regional availability of nutrition, while investments in the value-added chain can boost income and employment. But the negative cases of 'land grabbing' have highlighted the limitations and risks of major private commercial investments in structurally weak developing countries. Local people then have no benefits whatsoever—apart from the loss of their ancestral land.

The land-matrix supported by the BMZ creates transparency here. Since the year 2000, over 400 large-scale foreign land acquisitions or leases were registered covering an area of 10 million hectares in Africa. Most of these are now being farmed, but there is a declining number and scale of new land acquisitions. A much more widespread phenomenon, which attracts less attention, is domestic 'land grabbing' when local, often urban elites assert ownership rights over areas of land. The social and ecological sustainability of such investments largely depends on how they are organized. The basic political conditions must be arranged so that land grants are comprehensible and transparent as well as agricultural investments structured according to internationally recognized guidelines. This includes good land use planning and adequate participation of the local population with respect for their legitimate land rights—but unfortunately these are often non-formalized. The secure access to land is a basic condition for a world without hunger and the sustainable use of natural resources.

A decisive reason for the disappearance of trees in Africa was the soaring population growth. This also looks set to continue over the next decades—Africa is the only continent on earth where the population is still growing rapidly. Are the achievements of the FMNR method therefore not at risk of being destroyed?

Sooner or later, traditional forms of land use threaten the balance between the population and its needs as well as the resources that can be exploited with the available techniques and technologies. This situation has already begun in many countries in Africa and is expected to continue. Trees offer many products (for example, wood, honey, fruit, fodder for livestock and food stocks for periods of famine) as well as environmental services such as permanent water sources, improved micro-climate or prevention of soil erosion. Local people living in poverty in the rural regions particularly depend on the availability and access to these products and services.

The challenges for the conservation of trees, forests and productive landscapes matter less in relation to technical aspects than as to how societies plan to and can apply mandatory regulations for using these resources, or in other words how they evaluate what is culturally reasonable and enforceable. In addition to the protection of trees there is greater emphasis on measures for the restoration of forests and wooded, productive landscapes. Often, this involves highly labour-intensive measures that African states need.

Can any steps be taken to prevent rapid population growth?

There are educational programmes particularly for girls and women that we hope will lead to a reduction of population growth. Such programmes were already highly successful in some parts of Africa. Generally, the number of children falls as income rises. Previously, people had lots of children as security for old age. Nowadays, they tend to be associated with poverty in old age.

The strong population growth is also described as an economic opportunity for Africa: in contrast to Europe's ageing population the continent could profit from its very young population. Is population growth an opportunity or a threat?

In this case, I also regard the rumour of Africa as a continent of opportunity as misguided. People refer to a 'population dividend' because the growing population should lead to stronger economic growth, since more is being produced and consumed and state revenues rise. However, this supposed dividend rests on the assumption that the increasing population is also in employment and with food to eat. Currently, at least in Africa's case this does not apply. While the focus on the private sector and industrialization is appropriate, it will not resolve the problem of the lack of opportunities for many young African men and women. I believe that we all underestimate the true dimensions of this challenge. That's partly because we're too naive and approach Africa's countries from a Eurocentric standpoint. Partly because we don't want to accept the sheer scale of the problem and the highly conflicted ethnic dimension. And probably partly also because politicians are not happy to admit that they have no solution for a problem. If we were honest, we would again resort to the message about the paths that we would explore together as companions. Mutual trust would at least be a good starting point: the idea that the other party has kind intentions towards me because we're dependent on each other.

Will the successes achieved with the FMNR method also tend to stem the flow of migration?

This is part of an honest answer that I just mentioned: No. However, in Northern Ethiopia, in Tigray, we spoke with a family where the man could return from Saudi Arabia because the restoration of the valley allowed the people living there to secure their livelihoods again from their own farm products. Therefore, this is actually possible on a small scale.

FMNR is an amazingly simple solution for a pretty severe problem. Have you also already come across such simple solutions for complex problems in other areas of development policy?

I'm not at all sure that this is correct. Perhaps FMNR is the simple approach, however, it's difficult to realize.

At least, FMNR is cost effective. In development aid policy, the key factor is also the allocation of resources. In other words, one must spend the funds made available by the governments of industrialized nations. In this case, the method is certainly not helpful.

It's correct that especially in dry regions FMNR is comparatively extremely low cost. In these regions, the economic opportunities are generally also heavily restricted due to climate conditions and the lack of infrastructure; private investments tend to be unattractive here. FMNR would certainly gain even more attention in development policy, if these rural regions were a greater priority for the partner governments and the focus 'natural resources and rural development' played a more crucial role for the donors.

The extensive use of agro-forestry practices such as FMNR in Niger and other regions of the Sahel was also favoured because the population had a bigger say in farming the forestry resources. In Niger, the method spread very quickly and without complications across a vast area extending for several hundred kilometres. Studies concluded that specific soil qualities were particularly responsive there. In numerous regions of Africa, the conditions are possibly not so favourable. Therefore, it can take longer for FMNR to become effective. Besides, unclear ownership and property structures hamper its extension as well as the classic and outdated concepts of agricultural advisory services. I have no intention of disputing the fact that FMNR requires a form of consultancy that we're in no position to offer with our Western implementation agencies. Apprenticeships and dialogue with the local population require the prior training of many local facilitators. And the 'expats' perhaps also prefer active involvement in other projects where they do not have to travel across karstified valleys and in scorching sunshine. In connection with FMNR money is only required for labour and consultancy services. It's not even necessary to purchase trees; here, the outflow of funds in fact becomes a problem.

To be successful with the FMNR method in restoring degraded landscapes, no development aid is necessary at all—African smallholder farmers can also implement this without support. Is that typical for development aid in general whose benefits are more and more critically questioned?

I agree with you. However, please don't think that you could solve all of Africa's problems with the FMNR method and that only the West and Western aid are to blame for everything that doesn't work in Africa.

China has shown that helping Africa with economic cooperation on an equal level and substantial investments in infrastructure can work much better than individual aid projects. Has this led to a new approach in Western states?

The 'Partnership with Africa', which was launched in 2017 during the German G20 presidency, aims with a range of different programmes to strengthen the private sector in Africa and to attract international investors. Meanwhile, in the 'Compact with Africa' several African countries plan to improve the investment climate in their states to persuade investors to locate in the country. Three of these nations (Ivory Coast, Ghana and Tunisia) have additionally set up partnerships with the BMZ that are to bring forward reforms to improve the investment climate. Against the backdrop of the immense requirement for investment in Africa, the partners increasingly concentrate on a catalytic effect of their capital funds: taxation revenue should be used strategically to attract private investments.

Chancellor Angela Merkel said in November 2017 at the African Union–EU Summit in Abidjan, Ivory Coast, that we must advance 'from development cooperation to economic development'. You can call that learning from China, but it's also simply logical. After all, where should prosperity come from? Certainly not from foreign aid payments! We have a stake in Africa's well-being. Since neither we nor Africans have so far invented a totally new societal model for their continent, we will probably have to base our endeavour on the market economy like in other parts of the world.

In future, should one entirely dispense with development aid and instead take Africa more seriously as an economic partner?

I'm not convinced by radical changes of course. We must do lots of things better, though not do everything differently.

From the external perspective, the FMNR farmers could be helped best if a market were created for the products from their trees such as was the case, for example, with the shea tree and shea butter, which is produced from its seeds, or gum arabic. Do you see opportunities in this area?

Of course, there are great opportunities here but none of this creates millions of jobs. And the farmers must realize: everything that they produce must be offered on qualitative and price terms that encourage others to spend their valuable money on this. Subsidized projects due to development cooperation certainly don't achieve that.

If development is profitable, it asserts itself autonomously. Has development policy in the past placed too little emphasis on this principle?

You can debate numerous ideas about this as well. However, nobody should act as if he already knew how to do things better anyway.

The 21st century is occasionally described as the African century. Is that only PR hype or is there a grain of truth in it?

You can probably put it like that. But the truth is that this can also go very wrong. Then maybe it's still an African century, though not with the Asian connotation as a new dawn for a continent. Just consider the immense population growth that can also be a time bomb. Incidentally, it's also true that optimism is the only political error which is worthwhile.

Postscript

Tony Rinaudo

In his 1864 seminal book "Man and Nature", George Marsh wrote these haunting words: "There are parts of Asia Minor, of Northern Africa, of Greece, and even of Alpine Europe, where the operation of causes set in action by man has brought the face of the earth to a desolation almost as complete as that of the moon; and though, within that brief space of time which we call 'the historical period,' they are known to have been covered with luxuriant woods, verdant pastures, and fertile meadows ... A territory larger than all Europe, the abundance of which sustained in bygone centuries a population scarcely inferior to that of the whole Christian world at the present day, has been entirely withdrawn from human use, or, at best, is thinly inhabited."

This level of destruction had been attained by the time world population had reached slightly over 1.2 billion. Bulldozers had not yet been invented and no forest had been laid low through the insatiable appetite of the chainsaw. Today, we stand at a crossroads. The massive cloud bursts of deforestation, land degradation, climate change and population growth are converging into a perfect storm, moving inexorably towards us and poised to engulf all in its path.

Tanzanian farmer, Marimo Mbijima, once took me to the edge of his farm to show me a gnarled tree stump. The top of the stump was bowl shaped and blackened from years of repeated burning, but from the side sprung several sturdy stems which he was cultivating. It was a valued, but increasingly rare wild fruit-bearing tree. "This tree used to be my enemy," Marimo told me: "I burnt the stump every year to get rid of it. Since learning about FMNR it has become my friend, and I am so ashamed that I ever tried to kill it."

The world has long known that people need trees. At this critical point in history, it is now time to know, and to act on the fact that more than ever, trees need people, for the sake of the earth, and for the sake of all the earth's inhabitants, including human kind. It is time to move beyond comprehension of, and remorse for the damage we have done. It's time to act. Knowledge and sentiment will not save us from this impending peril of our own making. Fortunately, at the very moment when unparalleled action is called for, we have a tool commensurate to the task of countering the enormous challenges before us. It is time for decisive action.

What does FMNR represent for global land restoration? A 'phase change' comes close to describing it. Phase change occurs when dry ice changes directly from a solid to a gas without liquefying. Prior to the re-discovery of FMNR, landscape restoration was not cost effective, scalable or sustainable using conventional methods. We went from pushing, cajoling and incentivizing people to do what they should willingly and happily do for their own well-being, to witnessing a self-propelled movement we weren't even aware of its existence until it was later revealed through satellite imagery. We had no knowledge of, let alone control of what was happening. Now the floodgates have been opened.

The almost universal reaction to being introduced to FMNR is amazement. For many, for the first time, they catch a glimmer of hope for their own futures. Others marvel at what has been achieved in Niger despite the paltry starting point. And they ask: "If Nigeriens with minimum help living under such extreme conditions and starting with such a degraded landscape can turn their situation around—what about us? What can we achieve?" And the answer of course is: not only can you match what they achieved. Knowing what we know today you can do it even better, and do it faster.

The rapid transformation in Niger begs of the international community a similar question. If Niger, one of the world's poorest countries, with an extreme climate on the edge of the Sahara Desert, with minimal NGO and government interference or funding can restore 200 million trees on 5 million hectares over a 20-year period largely through a farmer-to-farmer movement, what do you think might be possible if all stakeholders—donors, scientists, governments, policy makers, business, NGOs, traditional and religious leaders and farmers—partnered and were serious about land restoration? Technically, there is no reason why simultaneously 5 million hectares of land could not be restored in multiple countries within five years.

Indeed, we are seeing the early stirrings of such an international movement, and a platform for the spread of FMNR is coming into being. For example, at the second African Drylands Week convened by the African Union in 2014, the following declaration was made: "(We) recommend and propose that the drylands development community, through the African Union, and all collaborating and supporting organizations, commit seriously to achieving the goal of enabling EVERY farm family and EVERY village across the drylands of Africa to be practicing FMNR and assisted natural regeneration by the year 2025." This represents an enormous vote of confidence by Africa's peak political body.

On a world scale, the Bonn Challenge, a global effort to bring 150 million hectares of the world's deforested and degraded land into restoration by 2020, and 350 million hectares by 2030, was launched in 2011. The Bonn Challenge was later endorsed and extended by the New York Declaration on Forests at the 2014 UN Climate Summit. In 2015, Africa set its own target towards meeting the Bonn challenge: the African Forest Landscape Restoration Initiative (AFR100), a country-led effort to bring 100 million hectares of deforested and degraded landscapes across Africa into restoration by 2030. In addition, the Great Green Wall of the Sahara and the Sahel Initiative is Africa's flagship scheme to combat the effects of climate change and desertification. Led by the African Union, the initiative aims to transform the lives of millions of people by creating a great mosaic of green and productive landscapes across North Africa, the Sahel and the Horn.

In January 2018, Global Good, a Bill & Melinda Gates funded research lab, facilitated a workshop, bringing together a group of international FMNR thought and action leaders along with scientists, Geographic Information System specialists, donors, publicists and academics to determine what was needed to "massively scale FMNR". Blockages and critical gaps in FMNR promotion and uptake were identified and an action plan was developed. This was the first time such a comprehensive international group of specialists have come together to plan how to create a global movement. I am confident that this workshop will ultimately result in far greater awareness and spread of FMNR.

Once barriers to the spread of FMNR have been identified and a strategy has been developed, resource mobilization on the scale of the Global Alliance for Vaccines and Immunization (GAVI) fund should be considered. GAVI created a mechanism to raise new resources for immunization and to swiftly channel them to developing country health systems. Total resource mobilization exceeded USD 1 billion for the 2001–2005 commitment period. Is it not worth an equal effort to restore the earth's life support system?

My hope is that this book will inspire new thinking and new action for the restoration of the earth's trees. I have been called many names such as 'crazy white farmer', 'tree whisperer' or 'the forest maker'—you can judge for yourselves what fits. For me, I am simply living a very blessed life. My child's prayer "use me somehow and somewhere to make a difference" has been and is being fulfilled beyond my wildest dreams. I thank God daily for the privilege to be of assistance in this way.

APPENDIX

BIBLIOGRAPHY

Friedrich Hölderlin: Poems and Fragments, trans. by Michael Hamburger, Cambridge, London, Cambridge University Press, 1980, p. 463.

Dennis Garrity "FMNR is Now a Widely Scaled-Up Agricultural Practice in the Drylands: A Robust Legacy of Tony Rinaudo's Career"

Akinnifesi, F., O. Ajayi, G. Sileshi, P. Chirwa, J. Chianu. 2010. Fertilizer tree systems for sustainable food security in the maize based production systems of East and Southern Africa Region: A review. Agronomy for Sustainable Development, 30: 615–629.

Barnes, R. and C. Fagg. 2003. Tropical Forestry Papers no. 41. 267pp. Oxford Forestry Institute (OFI). Oxford, UK.

Bayala, J., J. Sanou, Z. Teklahaimanot, A. Kalinganire, S. Oeudrago. 2014. Parklands for buffering climate risk and sustaining agricultural production in the Sahel of West Africa, Current Opinion in Environmental Sustainability, 6: 28–34.

Bayala, J., L.K. Heng, M. van Noordwijk and S.J. Ouedraogo. 2008. Hydraulic redistribution study in two native tree species of agroforestry parklands of West African dry savanna. Acta Oecologica – International Journal of Ecology 34: 370–378.

Beedy, T.L., G. Nyamadzawo, E. Luedeling, D-G. Kim, F. Place, K. Hadgu. 2014. Carbon Sequestration and Soil Fertility Replenishment by Agroforestry Technologies for Small Landholders of Eastern and Southern Africa. In: Managing Soils of Smallholder Agriculture, Rattan Lal and B.A. Stewart (eds), Boca Raton, Florida: CRC Press.

Boffa, J-M. 1999. Agroforestry Parklands in Sub-Saharan Africa, FAO Conservation Guide 34, Food and Agriculture Organization of the UN, Rome.

Bunch, R. 2012, pers. comm.

Campbell, B.M., S.J. Vermeulen, T. Lynam. 1991. Value of Trees in the Small-scale Farming Sector of Zimbabwe. IDRC, Ottawa, Canada.

Cervigni, R. and M. Morris (eds). 2016. Confronting drought in Africa's drylands: opportunities for enhancing resilience. Washington, DC: World Bank.

Chaïbou, Guéro. pers. comm.

Dewees, P. 1995. Trees on farms in Malawi: Private investment, public policy, and farmer choice. World Development 23: 1085–1102.

Engelstaedter, S., I. Tegen and R. Washington. 2006. North African dust emissions and transport. Earth Sciences Review (79): 73–100.

Francis, R. and P. Weston. 2015. The social, environmental and economic benefits of Farmer Managed Natural Regeneration (FMNR). World Vision Australia, Melbourne.

Garrity, D., F. Akinnifesi, O. Ajayi, G.W. Sileshi, J.G. Mowo, A. Kalin-Ganire, M. Larwanou and J. Bayala. 2010. Evergreen Agriculture: A robust approach to sustainable food security in Africa. Food Security. 2(3): 197–214.

Glenn, J.V. 2012. Economic Assessment of Landowner Incentives: Analyses in North Carolina and Malawi. PhD Dissertation. North Carolina State University, Raleigh, North Carolina.

Hadgu, K,J. Mowo, D. Garrity, G. Sileshi. 2011. Current extent of evergreen agriculture and prospects for improving food security and environmental resilience in Ethiopia. International Journal of Agriculture 1 (1).

Haglund, E., J. Ndjeunga, L. Snook and D. Pasternak. 2011. Dry land tree management for improved household livelihoods: farmer managed natural regeneration in Niger. J. Environ. Manage. 92: 1696–1705.

Hirai, M. 2005. A vegetation-maintaining system as a livelihood strategy among the Sereer, West-Central Senegal. African Study Monographs, Suppl. 30: 183–193, March 2005 183

Kundhlande et al. 2017. Taking to Scale Tree-Based Systems that Enhance Food Security, Improve Resilience to Climate Change, and Sequester Carbon In Malawi. PROFOR. World Bank: Washington DC.

Mayaux, P., E. Bartholome, S. Fritz and A. Belward. 2004. A new land-cover map of Africa for the year 2000. J. Biogeogr. 31: 861–877.

Monela G.C., S.A.O. Chamshama, R. Mwaipopo, D.M. Gamassa. 2005. A study on the social, economic and environmental impacts of forest landscape restoration in Shinyanga Region, Tanzania. A report for the Ministry of Natural Resources and Tourism and the World Conservation Union (IUCN).

Oginosako Z., P. Simitu, C. Orwa, S. Mathenge. 2006. Are they competing or compensating on farm? Status of indigenous and exotic tree species in a wide range of agro-ecological zones of Eastern and Central Kenya, surrounding Mt. Kenya. ICRAF Working Paper no. 16. Nairobi: World Agroforestry Centre.

Place, F., D. Garrity, S. Mohan and P. Agostini. 2016. Tree-Based Production Systems for Africa's Drylands. World Bank Studies. Washington, DC: World Bank.

Place, F. and J. Binam. 2013. Economic impacts of Farmer-Managed Natural Regeneration in the Sahel. End-of-Project Technical Report for Free University Amsterdam and IFAD; World Agroforestry Center, Nairobi, Kenya (mimeo).

Pullan, R.A. 1974. Farmed parkland in West Africa. Savanna, 3(2): 119–151.

Raison, J-P. 1988. Les parcs en Afrique: état des connaissances, perspectives de recherches. Document de travail. Paris, Centres d'Etudes Africaines, EHESS. 117pp.

Reij, C, D. Garrity. 2016. Scaling up farmer-managed natural regeneration in Africa to restore degraded landscapes. Biotropica 48(6): 834–843.

Reij, C., G. Tappan, and M. Smale. 2009. Agro-environmental transformation in the Sahel. IFPRI Discussion Paper, Washington 00914.

Reij, C., and R. Winterbottom. 2015. Scaling up regreening: six steps to success. A practical approach to forest and landscape restoration. Washington, WRI report. www.wri.org/sites/default/files/scaling-regreening-six-steps-success.pdf.

Romieu, I., J.J. Sienra-Monge, M. Ramirez-Aguilar, M.M. Tellez-Rojo, H. Moreno-Macias, N.I. Reyes-Ruiz, B.E. Del Rio-Navarro, M.X. Ruiz-Navarro, G. Hatch, R. Slade, M. Hernandez-Avila. 2002. Antioxidant supplementation and lung functions among children with asthma exposed to high levels of air pollutants, American Journal of Respiratory and Critical Care Medicine, 166(5): 703–709.

Shivdenko, A., C.V. Barber, R. Persson. 2005. Forest and woodland systems. In Millenium Ecosystem Assessment. Retrieved March 15, 2010, from www.millenniumassessment.org/documents/document.290.aspx.pdf

Shumba, A., B. Nyamasoka, P. Nyamugafata, S. Madyiwa, and J. Nyamangara. 2010. Effects of optimised innovative soil fertility and water management technologies on maize production in two contrasting soils in Harare, Zimbabwe. Second RUFORUM Biennial Regional Conference on "Building capacity for food security in Africa", Entebbe, Uganda, 20–24 September 2010: 651–657. RUFORUM.

Sileshi, G., F.K. Akinnifesi, O. C. Ajayi, F. Place. 2008. Meta-analysis of maize yield response to woody and herbaceous legumes in the sub-Saharan Africa. Plant Soil 307: 1–19.

Smith, K. R., C.F. Corvalán, T. Kiellström. 1999. How much global ill health is attributable to environmental factors? Journal of Epidemiology 10, 5: 573–584. www.who.int/environmental_information/Disburden/Articles/smith.pdf.

Smith, E. 2010. Local knowledge of natural regeneration and tree management in Sahelian parklands north of Tominian Mali. MSc thesis, School of Environment, Natural Resources and Geography, University of Bangor, Wales.

Tappan, G. 2016. US Geological Survey, pers. Comm.

Tougiani, A., C. Guero, and T. Rinaudo. 2009. Community mobilization for improved livelihoods through tree crop management in Niger. Geoforum 74: 377–389.

Winterbottom, R., C. Reij, D. Garrity, J. Glover, D. Hellums, M. McGahuey,

S. Scherr. 2013. Improving land and water management. Working Paper. World Resources Institute: 44.

Yamba, B., and M.N. Sambo. 2012. La régénération naturelle assistée et la securité alimentaire des méages de 5 terroirs villageois des départements de Kantche et Mirriah (région de Zinder, Niger). Report for the International Fund for Agricultural Development. Etude FIDA 1246-VU University Amsterdam.

LIST OF PHOTOS AND DIAGRAMS

> © Johannes Dieterich: *Cover*; p. 34 (above), 35, 36f., 38 (above), 39, 44, 45, 48, 49 (above)
> © Saskia Noll: Drawing: p. 12–15; p. 120: Table 1 [Source: R. Winterbottom et al. 2013]
> Silas Koch, © World Vision: p. 46, 47 (above), 49 (below)
> © World Vision: p. 34 (below), 38 (below), 40–43, 47 (below)
> © Mark Lewis: p. 149

ABOUT THE AUTHORS

Johannes Dieterich (b. 1957) has reported for more than 20 years from Johannesburg as the Africa correspondent for several German language newspapers and magazines like Berliner Zeitung, Frankfurter Rundschau, brandeins (Hamburg) and profil (Vienna). He has to cover no less than 50 African countries, some of which he still has to explore first-hand. The reporter first met Tony Rinaudo in Somalia in April 2016, afterwards also accompanying the 'forest-maker' to Ethiopia and Niger.

The native Swabian from the abbey town of Maulbronn studied theology and history. After graduation, Dieterich turned to journalism. He spent several years working for television and print media, before being drawn to South Africa following Nelson Mandela's release. His book "South Africa" was released last year by the Berlin publisher Ch. Links-Verlag. He is married to the South African Merle Dieterich and has two children.

Dennis Garrity (b. 1952) is a systems agronomist and research leader whose career has focused on the development of small-scale farming systems in the tropics. He has served as Drylands Ambassador for the UN Convention to Combat Desertification, emphasizing the role of agroforestry, evergreen agriculture and landcare as critical to sustainable land management.

Garrity studied agriculture and agronomy in the US state of Ohio and the Philippines and obtained his PhD in crop physiology at the University of Nebraska. He served as Director General of the World Agroforestry Centre (ICRAF), Nairobi, from 2001 to 2011. Currently, he is chairing the global initiative to create an EverGreen Agriculture Partnership, anticipating the transformation of African and Asian farming through the integration of trees into farming systems and upscaling the practices of Evergreen Agriculture to tens of millions of smallholder farmers. He is married to Vilma Caluya Garrity and has two children.

Günter Nooke (b. 1959) has been German Chancellor Angela Merkel's Personal Representative for Africa since 2010, and Commissioner for Africa in the German Federal Ministry for Economic Cooperation and Development (BMZ) since 2014. In this capacity, he has already visited more than thirty African countries—many of these several times. He represents the German Federal Government at national and international events concerning Africa; he also publishes on the subject as well as giving frequent media interviews.

Nooke obtained a degree in physics in Leipzig and belonged to the Christian opposition in the GDR. He is a co-founder of Democratic Awakening (Demokratischer Aufbruch), and in 1990 was a member of the East German Central Round Table. Six years later, he joined the CDU and from 1998 to 2005 represented the party in the German Bundestag. In 2006, the civil rights activist was appointed the Federal Government Commissioner for Human Rights Policy and Humanitarian Aid. As this position was assigned to the FDP under the new coalition, in March 2010 Nooke was appointed the German Chancellor's Personal Representative for Africa.

Tony Rinaudo (b. 1957). After gaining a Bachelor of Rural Science at the University of New England, Australia, Tony Rinaudo spent 18 years in Niger Republic as manager of the Maradi Integrated Development Project (1981 to 1999). His activities contributed to a transformation in the way Nigeriens farm, and to the reforestation of around seven million hectares of land. Today, the 'Niger Phenomenon' serves as an inspiration to re-greening movements globally. For his service to humanity and contribution to the environment, the government of Niger awarded him its highest honour for an expatriate, the Merite Agricole du Niger.

Rinaudo joined World Vision Australia in 1999, starting off as a programme officer for Ethiopia and Kenya. He initiated and oversaw several landmark projects and is currently the Principal Natural Resources advisor for World Vision Australia. His work has contributed significantly to greater international awareness of the impact and efficacy of reforestation. He is married to Liz and has four children.

www.ingramcontent.com/pod-product-compliance
Lightning Source LLC
Chambersburg PA
CBHW020853160426
43192CB00007B/911